10-MINUTE IDEAS FOR EARLY YEARS

D0231476

Circle time

Linda Mort

■ **Quick activities for any time of the day**

■ **Links to Early Learning Goals** ■ **Time-saving photocopiables**

Credits

Author
Linda Mort

Editor
Susan Howard

Assistant Editor
Jennifer Shiels

Series Designer
Anna Oliwa

Designer
Andrea Lewis

Cover Illustration
Craig Cameron/Art Collection

Illustrations
Cathy Hughes

Text © 2004
© 2004 Scholastic Ltd

Designed using Adobe InDesign

Published by Scholastic Ltd
Villiers House
Clarendon Avenue
Leamington Spa
Warwickshire
CV32 5PR

www.scholastic.co.uk

Printed by Bell & Bain Ltd, Glasgow

2 3 4 5 6 7 8 9   4 5 6 7 8 9 0 1 2 3

British Library Cataloguing-in-Publication Data
A catalogue record for this book is available from the British Library.

ISBN 0-439-97114-4

Contents

Contents

Introduction

This book provides ideas for adults in all early years settings to maximise their use of time through 10-minute circle time activities. The circle time format is used as a collaborative and supportive framework for a wide variety of simple and enjoyable activities developing self-esteem and team-building skills across all six areas of learning, as outlined in the *Curriculum Guidance for the Foundation Stage* (QCA). The activities can be incorporated as part of a planned curriculum or used in occasional 'pockets of time', as required. The ideas aim to bring an original or unusual twist to activities within popular early years themes.

Using the activities

The circle time experiences are designed to be varied in approach and easy to carry out, requiring the minimum of resources and little or no preparation. Many feature rhymes, songs and physical activities. They are ideal for use as an introduction to a theme or at the end of a theme as a way of reminding the children about what they have learned. At the beginning of each activity, remind children about the three 'rules': taking turns, listening to each other and being able to 'pass', if any child wishes to do so. It is beneficial for any adults involved to be at the same level as everyone else, whether on the floor or on chairs, and to participate as a member of the circle in order to encourage shy or younger children, and to model language.

Planning for the Stepping Stones and Early Learning Goals

When drawing up short- or medium-term plans, aim for a wide coverage of the Stepping Stones and Early Learning Goals within your chosen theme.

The circle time activities in this book can be easily incorporated into your planning. The 60 ideas are divided into the six Areas of Learning, and each activity includes Learning Objectives, broken down into Stepping Stones and Early Learning Goals. You can easily adapt the thematic focus of each activity to fit any theme in your planning, by retaining the format of the activity but adapting the vocabulary and any items used. For example, in 'The hungry duck' activity on page 30, the duck swimming around a pond eating crumbs of bread could become a shoe-box aeroplane flying around the world, picking up play people passengers.

At the end of each activity idea, there are bullet-pointed 'Further ideas', which provide suggestions for ways of developing the circle time activities across a range of Areas of Learning. The circle time activities are also useful when planning reinforcement or development 'next step' experiences for individuals or small groups of children, based on your observation of their learning needs and interests.

Assessing the activities

Circle time provides an ideal opportunity for assessing the progress, interests and needs of individuals or small groups of children, across the whole of the Foundation Stage curriculum. Children's personal, social and emotional  development can be assessed by observing how they co-operate, share and join in. Language skills can be assessed by noting how well children listen to others, understand instructions and express themselves in discussion. In terms of mathematical development, many circle time experiences offer opportunities for assessing counting skills and spatial awareness. Children's awareness of the wider world can be observed by their level of engagement in circle time activities, including sensory exploration and the natural and built environment, and the world of work. Circle time provides opportunities for observing and assessing children's individual physical development, and their ability to move within a group. Levels of creative development can be noted through role-play, imaginative discussion and the ability to think of alternative ideas. If possible, it is helpful to have another adult involved at circle time, to assist in observing and assessing children.

Multicultural links

Many circle time activities can be given a multicultural dimension by inviting in a parent or visitor to join the circle, and by substituting words from other languages, or by using objects from other countries, such as items of clothing or food.

Setting up the environment

For all of the activities, you will need a clear, safe space, either indoors or outdoors. If indoors, a carpeted area is ideal, so everyone can sit on the floor. If children are new to circle time, it is helpful to chalk a circle, using tailor's chalk. Alternatively, use carpet squares. Each idea in the book includes information on organising the children at the beginning of the activity. Sometimes this will involve the use of children's chairs. If carrying out the activities outside, chalk a circle on the playground.

How to use this book

To find an activity to suit your needs, either locate an appropriate Stepping Stone or Early Learning Goal, or choose an activity that fits in with one of your themes or one that can be adapted (see Planning for the Stepping Stones and Early Learning Goals, above). Each activity includes a list of items required, under 'What you need' and a description of any necessary preparation. This is followed by a 'What to do' section and a 'Support and extension' section, which provides suggestions for simplifying the activity for younger or less able children, and extending it for older children.

There are bullet-pointed 'Further ideas' for cross-curricular development, followed by suggestions for involving families in 'Home links'. At the end of the book, there are 14 photocopiable pages: suggestions for using them within the circle time activities, and for children's use at another time or at home, are given in the related activities.

Personal, social and emotional development

The activities in this chapter focus on how children can build relations with peer groups, develop an awareness of their own and other peoples views and feelings and become more sensitive to these, and to consider the consequences of their actions.

Circle of friends

What you need
Two pieces of thick wool in contrasting colours, approximately 20cm in length; one piece of wool, approximately 10cm in length; two pieces of wool, approximately 4m in length; tape measure; scissors; five chairs.

Preparation
Knot the two 20cm pieces of wool together at one end. Twist them around each other, then knot the other end. Secure the ends together with the 10cm piece of wool to make a rakhi bracelet. Knot the ends of a 4m piece of wool together to make a large loop. Cut the other 4m piece of wool into five lengths, approximately 80cm, for each child.

What to do
Ask each child to sit on a chair in a circle. Show the children the rakhi bracelet and tell them about the festival of Raksha Bandhan. Explain that Hindu girls make bracelets to give to their brothers to show how much they care about them.

Place the large loop of wool on the children's laps. Stand next to a child and tie the end of their length of wool on to the loop, where it lies on their lap. Show each child how to hold the large loop in their right hand (or left hand) and wind the other piece of wool 'over and over' the loop with their left hand (or right hand) so that it looks 'twisted'. Knot the piece of wool to the loop when it has been wound. Then ask the children to sit with their hands underneath the 'bracelet' and to say something positive about the child sitting next to them, for example, 'I like it when you share the crane with me'.

Support and extension
Let younger children talk about something they can see on the child sitting next to them, such as 'I like your shoes'. Ask older children to talk positively about someone who is not present.

■ ■

Further idea
■ Make a wall display with the large rakhi and invite the children to draw pictures of each other to put inside.

LEARNING OBJECTIVES
STEPPING STONE
Relate and make attachments to members of their group.

EARLY LEARNING GOAL
Form good relationships with adults and peers.

GROUP SIZE
Five children.

HOME LINKS
Let the children make individual rakhis to take home as gifts.

Teddy's feelings

What you need
One teddy bear; one copy of the 'How is Teddy?' photocopiable sheet on page 67; scissors; three straws; sticky tape; tray.

Preparation
Cut out the individual teddy bear faces on the sheet. Stick a straw at the back of each one with sticky tape and put them on the tray.

What to do
Gather together in a circle on the carpet. Talk about how we can tell how somebody is feeling by looking at the expression on their face. Introduce the children to Teddy, and then show them each of the cut-out faces in turn. Say that you want to find out how Teddy is feeling today.

Pass the bear around the circle as the children sing the song 'Teddy's feelings' on the sheet. Each time the song ends, ask the child who is holding the bear to pick a cut-out face from the tray. Encourage them to hold the cut-out in front of Teddy, and say: 'Teddy is feeling… because…'.

Support and extension
Ask younger children only to say how Teddy is feeling, but not why. With older children, remove the tray and put Teddy in the centre of the circle. Ask the children to clap and sing, 'What makes Teddy scared, giggly or shy?'. Every time the song finishes, ask each child to hold the bear and to explain why Teddy would feel scared, giggly or shy.

Further ideas
■ Sing the song about children in your group. Clap as you sing, 'What makes… (child's name) feel happy, sad or cross?', then at the end of the song, ask the child concerned to say what would make them feel happy, sad or cross.

■ Put Teddy in the centre and describe a sad scenario. For example, 'Teddy was feeling sad because he had taken his friend Eddy's train, and now Eddy was sad, too'. Ask any child who has a solution to take the bear and say, 'Teddy should…'.

■ Ask the children to pretend to be bears at a teddy bears' picnic. Ask them to show you what expressions the bears might make as they prepare for, and then enjoy, the picnic. Provide safety mirrors for the children to practise their expressions in.

Elephants never forget

What you need
Strip of grey paper, approximately 50cm by 6cm (or an Alice band); one sheet
of grey paper, approximately 42cm by 21cm; pen; scissors; sticky tape.

Preparation
Fold the sheet of paper in half and draw a large semi-circular 'elephant's ear'.
Cut out to make two 'ears' and attach to the strip of paper (or Alice band) with
sticky tape. Tape the ends of the strip together to make a headband.

What to do
Gather together into a circle on the carpet. Explain to the children that some
people say that elephants are good at remembering things because they listen
carefully. Say that when people care about one another, they listen carefully to
find out special and important things about each other, so that they can make
one another happy.

Tell the children that you are going to play a game. In which everyone must
listen carefully to what the rest of the group says. Say that one person at a
time is going to be a special
'listening elephant' who says
what they remember hearing.
Begin by saying, 'My favourite
food is…'. Ask everyone
in turn to say what their
favourite food is. At the end of
the 'round' ask for a volunteer
'listening elephant' and let
them put on the elephant
ears. Invite them to name
one or more of the children
and their favourite food. Ask
for further volunteers and
play the game again using a
different favourite thing.

**LEARNING
OBJECTIVES**
STEPPING STONE
Have a sense of
belonging.

**EARLY LEARNING
GOAL**
Have a developing
awareness of their
own needs, views
and feelings and
be sensitive to the
needs, views and
feelings of others.

GROUP SIZE
Five or six children.

Support and extension
For younger children, reduce the number in the group. With older children,
increase the number of children or ask the 'elephants' to try remembering
everyone's favourite things.

Further ideas
■ Ask each child to name the different people in their family. See if an
'elephant' can remember the details for one or more children.
■ Ask the children to name things that they dislike.
■ Play 'It doesn't matter!'. After a 'round', ask for an 'elephant' to say, for
example, 'Mia said her favourite food is apples. I love bananas instead. It
doesn't matter!'.

HOME LINKS
Let each child make
a pair of 'ears' on a
paper band, to wear
as they play 'Listen
and remember' at
home. One person
recounts a list of
animals seen at the
zoo, while the other
person wears the
'ears' and repeats the
list. One more 'item'
is added each time.

Hello circle

What you need
Cassette or CD player; medium-paced music.

What to do
Ask six children to hold hands and stand in a small circle. Encourage them to drop hands and turn around so that they face outwards. Ask another six children to form an outer circle, not holding hands, with each child facing inwards, towards the original circle of children. Now play the music and ask the inner circle to move around sideways in one direction, while the outer circle moves in the opposite direction. (If necessary, have an adult in each circle to make sure that the circles move in the correct direction.)

Stop the music and ask the children to stop so they are facing a new partner. Ask the outside circle of children to say to their partners, 'Hello… (child's name), my name is… (child's name)'. Ask the inside circle to reply, 'Hello… (child's name), my name is… (child's name)'. Start and stop the music again, this time asking the inner circle to speak first. Restart the music four more times, asking the circles to begin speaking alternately.

Support and extension
For younger children, reduce the number in the group and use chairs so that they stop directly opposite another child when the music stops. Ask them to only say, 'Hello… (name of partner)'. Ask older children to say their first and last names, and possibly their middle names if they have one.

Further ideas
■ Instead of saying, 'Hello', let the children say, 'Good morning', 'Good afternoon', 'Good evening' or 'Good night'.
■ Let the children shake hands, saying, 'Hello, I'm…'.
■ Ask the children to say, 'Hello, how are you?', responding with, 'Very well, thank you. How are you?', and, finally, 'Fine, thank you'.
■ Ask the children to pretend to be elephants, greeting one another by shaking 'trunks' (arms).
■ Let the children use glove puppets to say, 'Hello'.

Round the garden

What you need
An artificial flower; watering can; doll's buggy; one A3 sized sheet of orange paper; sticky tape; two A3 sized sheets of green paper; six autumn leaves (real or paper); one child's broom; several pieces of clean 'litter'; waste bin.

Preparation
Stick the orange paper over the buggy to make it resemble a 'lawn mower'.

What to do
Sit the children in a circle. In the centre of the circle, the 'garden', make two groups of items:
- the flower, the sheets of green paper to represent 'grass', the leaves and the 'litter'
- the watering can, 'lawn mower' and waste bin.

Talk to the children about how and why gardens need to be looked after. Say that the bear in 'Round and round the garden' always looked after his garden. Let one child at a time be the 'bear' who walks round the 'garden' as the rest of the group say:

> *Round and round the garden*
> *Goes... (child's name) Bear,*
> *Working very hard indeed,*
> *Everywhere!*

At the end of the rhyme, ask the child to stand next to one item from the first group, such as 'litter', and then choose one item from the second group to deal with it, for example, the waste bin. Ask the 'bear' to talk about what they are doing.

Play the game several times, letting the children take turns to choose different items and ways of dealing with them.

Support and extension
Prompt younger children by asking, for example, 'What do you need to cut the grass?'. Ask older children what might happen if you did not cut the grass, water the flowers or pick up the litter and leaves.

Further ideas
- Instead of a garden, pretend the space is a house, farmyard or zoo, using home corner furniture or toy animals. Ask the 'bears' to mime being a spring-cleaner, farmer or zoo-keeper.
- Play 'Pass the spring-cleaning bowl'. Pass around a plastic washing-up bowl containing spring cleaning items. When the music stops, one child must remove an item, and talk about and demonstrate its use.

LEARNING OBJECTIVES
STEPPING STONE
Show care and concern for others, for living things and the environment.

EARLY LEARNING GOAL
Consider the consequences of their words and actions for themselves and others.

GROUP SIZE
Eight children.

HOME LINKS
Ask families to tell you about household chores with which their children help. Make an illustrated chart to display.

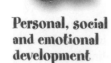

Friendly puppet

What you need

A glove puppet; six trays; one toy train engine; two pieces of train track; one book; three small building blocks; one very simple jigsaw; one small ball; four beads on a lace.

What to do

Sit together in a circle on the carpet. Introduce the puppet to the children, and say that it would like to be the children's friend. Explain that, when friends play together, they think about one another so that everyone can have fun. Say that the puppet does not understand yet how to do this, so you would like the children's help.

Give each child a tray. Put the engine and tracks on the first tray, and the open book on the second tray. Ask the third child to make a brick tower and the fourth child to do the jigsaw on their tray. Ask the fifth child to roll the ball around the tray and the sixth child to thread the beads. Hold up the puppet, approach the first child and 'make' the puppet gently take the train away from the child. Invite the group to say why this was wrong, and to suggest examples of what the puppet should have said and done.

Give the puppet to a child and ask them to re-enact the scenario, incorporating the group's ideas. Let everyone say, 'Well done...! (name of puppet)' and hug the puppet if they wish.

Continue around the group, pretending that the puppet takes the book, knocks over the tower, removes some jigsaw pieces, takes the ball and finally the beads. Repeat each scenario with a child holding a puppet and showing how it could behave correctly, for example, asking for a turn or suggesting working together.

Support and extension

Before playing the game with younger children, let two adults act out all of the scenarios for the children to watch. Ask older children to tell you about other children who have played in a friendly way with them.

Further ideas

■ Use play people and small-world toys to focus on other scenarios. Tell the children that one play person is 'learning how to play'.
■ Ask the children to make up rules for your setting.
■ Let individual children carry a puppet around your setting and report back to you, describing the puppet's progress in learning how to play.

What did I make?

What you need
One example from each child of artwork or a model, each using a different technique, for example, a play dough model on a board, painting, construction toy model, drawn or crayoned picture or pattern, threaded bead necklace, bucket sand pie on a tray, box model.

What to do
Put the items on the floor and sit the children around them. Ask everyone to look quietly and carefully at their own item. Choose one child and ask them to mime what they did to make their item. Ask the rest of the children to put up their hands if they can guess which item the child made. Continue until everyone has had a turn.

Support and extension
With younger children, call the game 'I can do that'. Use toys, each requiring distinctive hand or arm movements, for example, a ball, a book, a doll or bear wrapped in a blanket, a car, a teacup and saucer, a few small bricks, a dressing-up tabard and a pegboard. Ask everyone to choose an item without telling anyone and then mime how to use it. Play 'What did I use?' with older children. Ask everyone to name the things they used to make their item and see if the rest of the group can identify it.

■ ■ ■ ■ ■ ■ ■ ■ ■ ■ ■ ■ ■ ■ ■

Further ideas
■ Play 'I can do that outside'. Sit everyone in a circle on grass, or on chairs, with a selection of outdoor toys, such as a bicycle, scooter, ball, bat, skipping rope, small-world swing, slide, see-saw or climbing frame.
■ Play 'First and then', asking everyone to describe what they had to do to produce their artwork or model. For example, 'First I got two boxes, then I glued them together, then I painted them'.
■ Play 'Pairs' with an even number of children. Using pairs of items such as a paintbrush and empty pot, or a bucket and spade, give one item to each child, then ask them to find their 'partner'.

LEARNING OBJECTIVES
STEPPING STONE
Demonstrate a sense of pride in own achievement.

EARLY LEARNING GOAL
Select and use activities and resources independently.

■ ■ ■ ■ ■ ■ ■ ■ ■ ■

GROUP SIZE
Any size.

■ ■ ■ ■ ■ ■ ■ ■ ■

HOME LINKS
Play 'I can do this at home'. Ask families to help their children learn to mime a skill they have been practising, such as brushing their teeth or getting dressed. Back at your setting, let the children mime their skill for the rest of the group to guess.

Musical clothes

What you need
Four painting or waterplay aprons or tabards with Velcro fastenings; cassette or CD player; medium-paced music.

What to do
Ask four children to stand in a circle. Ask the rest of the group to form a circle, surrounding the four children in the inner circle. Encourage each child from the outer circle to stand behind one child from the inner circle. Now ask each child from the inner circle to turn their heads to see who their 'partner' is, then to face the centre again.

Give each child from the outer circle an apron or tabard to hold. Start the music and ask each circle to move round and to stop when the music stops. Explain that if any child from the inner circle has stopped in front of (or close to) their 'partner', they can turn around to face them. Ask the outer partner to put the apron or tabard on their inner partner and fasten it. Ask each 'dressed' child to sit down with their partner and watch as the remaining children continue to play. Reverse the roles and play the game again.

Support and extension
Let younger children use hats and scarves. With older children, ask each child in the outer circle to hold open a coat belonging to one of the children in the inner circle. When the music stops, ask any child in the inner circle who has stopped in front of (or close to) their coat, to slip their arms backwards and into their coat. Ask them to turn around and face their partner, who has to fasten the coat.

Further ideas
■ Instead of aprons, play the game with mittens or gloves.
■ Alternatively, use very loose jumpers with wide necks.

LEARNING OBJECTIVES
STEPPING STONE
Operate independently within the environment and show confidence in linking up with others for support and guidance.

EARLY LEARNING GOAL
Dress and undress independently and manage their own personal hygiene.

GROUP SIZE
Eight children.

HOME LINKS
Dress a bear in jumper, trousers, socks, shoes and coat. Position the bear where families can see it. Attach a label saying, 'I am learning how to dress myself. Please tell me if you are, too'. Whenever a parent says that their child has learned how to manage an item of clothing, let the child demonstrate their new skill to others.

A matter of taste

What you need
One vegetable rack (on casters) or a basket; selection of vegetables or fruit.

What to do
Put the vegetables in the rack or the fruit in the basket. Explain to the children that not all people like to eat the same kinds of vegetables or fruit, and that this does not matter. Say that it is very interesting to find out what other people like and do not like, because we can learn about trying vegetables and fruits that we might not have tasted before.

Ask the children to move the rack, or pass the basket, around the circle as they sing the following song to the tune of 'The Farmer's in the Den' (Traditional):

> *We all like different vegetables (or fruits)*
> *We all like different vegetables (or fruits)*
> *It's so interesting*
> *That we all like different vegetables (or fruits).*

Each time the song has ended, ask the child with the rack or basket to select an item, try to name it, and say, whether they like it or not, whether they like it a lot or a little, or whether they have not tried it yet. Ask each child to replace their item and then sing the song again. Tell the children that they may choose an item that someone else has already chosen, if they wish.

Support and extension
Ask younger children to say only whether or not they like an item. Invite older children to select an item that they are 'getting used to', or have 'changed their mind' about, for example, something that they previously didn't like but are now finding that they enjoy!

Further ideas
■ Use small variety packs of breakfast cereal.
■ Place a variety of boxed table games (each secured with an elastic band) inside the rack.
■ Arrange books in the rack or cut-out pictures of indoor and outdoor toys from catalogues, mounted on cards, in the basket.
■ Make bar charts of the children's favourite items.

LEARNING OBJECTIVES
STEPPING STONE
Make connections between different parts of their life experience.

EARLY LEARNING GOAL
Understand that people have different needs, views, cultures and beliefs, that need to be treated with respect.

GROUP SIZE
Whole group.

HOME LINKS
Place the vegetable rack or fruit basket in the entrance of your setting. Encourage the children to ask the person who collects them which items they like or dislike.

I know about that!

LEARNING OBJECTIVES
STEPPING STONE
Have an awareness of, and show interest and enjoyment in, cultural and religious differences.

EARLY LEARNING GOAL
Understand that they can expect others to treat their needs, views, cultures and beliefs with respect.

GROUP SIZE
Six to eight children.

What you need
A copy of the 'Festival facts' photocopiable sheet on page 68 for each child, and one for yourself; felt-tipped pen; scissors; drawstring bag; cassette or CD player; medium-paced music.

Preparation
On the children's photocopiable sheets write the name of a festival that you are currently finding out about, in the space after the word 'At'. Cut out the pictures on your photocopiable and place them in the drawstring bag.

What to do
Plan this activity for a session at the end of a theme about a particular festival or festivals. Sit the children in a circle and give each child the photocopiable sheet. Talk through the pictures together, saying, for example, 'Who can tell us about a special thing that people do at Eid?'. Collect the sheets back in.

Now play the music and pass the bag around the circle. When the music stops, ask the child holding the bag to reach inside and pick out a picture. Help them to ask the rest of the group the question that is based on their picture, for example, 'How do we greet people at Eid?'. Ask volunteers to speak one at a time. Accept general answers such as 'Happy Eid', and offer the suggestion of 'Eid Mubarak'. Encourage children who have celebrated the festival at home to say what they did. Ask the original child to replace the picture for use again before continuing the game.

Support and extension
With younger children, reduce the number of players to four. Sit together on the floor and put a sheet in front of each child, with four counting blocks. Say, 'Who can remember where people go to pray at Christmas?'. When the children have answered, ask everyone to cover the relevant picture with a block. Ask older children to talk about any stories related to a particular festival.

HOME LINKS
Let the children take the photocopiable sheets home to talk about with their families.

Further ideas
■ Decorate a dolls' house for a particular festival and put play dough festival food on the tables.
■ Position a teddy bear near the entrance and invite the children to use a relevant festival greeting, such as 'Happy Divali', or 'Kung Hey Fat Choi!' as they enter the setting.

Communication, language and literacy

This chapter helps the children to use body language as part of communication, extend their vocabulary and take turns during conversation, read simple sentences independently and attempt to write down more complex words phonetically.

Ring on a string

What you need
One piece of thick string, 3m long; one ring.

Preparation
Thread the string through the ring and knot the ends of the string together.

What to do
Stand five children in a circle, holding the string. Ask the sixth child to stand outside the circle, with their back to it. Invite everyone standing in the circle to pass the ring along the string, while singing the following song, to the tune of 'Where, oh Where has My Little Dog Gone?' (Traditional):

> *Where, oh where has the little ring gone?*
> *Oh where, oh where can it be?*
> *Look very closely at someone's face*
> *Then you may be able to see.*

At the end of the song, ask everyone to make 'two fists', around the string, with one child hiding the ring. Tell this child to smile and everyone else to keep a straight face. Then invite the sixth child to creep into the centre of the circle and guess who has the ring by looking for a smile.

Support and extension
With younger children, ask the person hiding the ring to close their eyes. With older children, sit them in pairs prior to the game and ask the first pair to 'signal' by twitching their noses, the second pair by opening their eyes wide and the third pair by pursing their lips. When the sixth child is in the circle, tell them to look at their partner's face. If their partner has the ring, ask them to 'signal'.

Further ideas
■ Let the children 'mirror' each other's body language and facial expressions.
■ Talk about animals' body language. Let the children complete the 'How do you feel?' photocopiable sheet on page 69.

Story song circle

LEARNING OBJECTIVES

STEPPING STONE
Listen to favourite nursery rhymes, stories and songs. Join in with repeated refrains, anticipating key events and important phrases.

EARLY LEARNING GOAL
Listen with enjoyment, and respond to stories, songs and other music, rhymes and poems and make up their own stories, songs, rhymes and poems.

GROUP SIZE
Whole group.

What you need
One copy of the 'Sing a song' photocopiable sheet on page 70 or page 71; notepad; pen.

What to do
Stand the children in a circle and sing the song 'There was a princess long ago' (Traditional), if the children are familiar with it. Let one child be the 'princess', in the middle of the circle. Encourage everyone to join in with the actions. At the end of the song invite everyone to sit down, still in a circle. Ask them to help you make up another story song circle about, for example, 'Little Red Riding Hood'. Say that everyone can sing the story and mime the actions. Ask the children what Little Red Riding Hood did first of all, and then invite them to suggest some actions to accompany the words.

Talk through the story, asking all of the group to practise the appropriate actions. Use the words on the photocopiable sheet as a guide or, ideally, use the children's own words. Write these down on a notepad. At the end of the 'rehearsal', ask everyone to stand up, choose a child to be Little Red Riding Hood in the centre of the circle, and begin your song. Choose other children to join Little  Red Riding Hood in the centre at appropriate parts of the song, for example, when she visits Grandma or when the wolf chases her.

Support and extension
With younger children, hold up pictures from fairy-tale books to prompt them about events in the stories. Ask older children to suggest other fairy-tales or stories to use for story song circles, such as 'Jack and the Beanstalk' or 'Goldilocks and The Three Bears'.

Further ideas
■ Use 'real-life' events about children and adults at your setting. Instead of singing 'Long ago', substitute the words 'yes there was', or 'yes he (she) did'.
■ Tell story song circles based on stories that the children have made up about soft toys or television characters.

HOME LINKS
Let each child take home a copy of one of the photocopiable song sheets (or similar versions) to sing and mime with their families.

Magic binoculars

What you need
Pair of toy binoculars (or kitchen roll tube, scissors and sticky tape); black felt-tipped pen; cassette or CD player; medium-paced music.

Preparation (if required)
Cut the tube in half and join with sticky tape to make a pair of 'binoculars'. Draw a line close to one end of the tubes to indicate the 'front'.

What to do
Stand together in a circle and invite one child to stand in the centre. Hold up the toy or 'home-made' binoculars and talk about how everything looks big if the binoculars are held the normal way, or small if they are held back-to-front.

Give the binoculars to the child in the centre of the circle. Play the music and ask everyone to move sideways until the music stops. Ask the child to hold the binoculars either way and to look at another child in the circle. Encourage the child with the binoculars to say whether they are holding them the 'normal' way or back-to-front. Now invite them to ask the second child to be a 'very big' or 'very small' animal or person. Say, for example, 'You look very small, Yaniv. Please be a tiny elf sewing shoes'. The second child should stand in the centre and carry out the instructions for everyone to copy. Then ask the first child to give the binoculars to the next child to continue the game.

Support and extension
Ask younger children only to be tall or small animals. Ask older children to be different types of insects.

Further ideas
■ Play 'Magic telescopes', using a toy telescope or a kitchen roll tube. Ask the centre child to be a ship's captain who spies a person or animal doing something on a desert island.
■ Ask the centre child to be a pilot or an astronaut who spies someone flying an aeroplane or rocket to… (name of country or planet).
■ Ask the centre child to open an alphabet book at any page and 'spy' someone whose name begins with the same sound. That child must carry out an action based on the picture on the page. For example, 'I spy someone whose name begins with a 'D' sound. Please pretend to be a dog'.

LEARNING OBJECTIVES
STEPPING STONE
Respond to simple instructions.

EARLY LEARNING GOAL
Sustain attentive listening, responding to what they have heard by relevant comments, questions or actions.

GROUP SIZE
Up to 15 children.

HOME LINKS
Let the children make magic binoculars or a telescope to take home, and use them to 'magic' family members into big or little creatures!

Can you cover?

What you need

Tray; small toy for each child (such as a toy animal or plastic food item); small piece of paper for each child (large enough to partially cover an individual item on the tray).

What to do

Sit together in a circle on the carpet and place the tray of items in the centre. Give each child a piece of paper. Encourage the first child to look at all of the items on the tray and to choose one without telling anyone what it is. Invite the child to choose only an item that they can name. Now, ask them to say to the child who is sitting next to them, 'Can you cover the…?'. Encourage the second child to partially cover the item with their piece of paper.

Next, invite the second child to choose an item and continue the game around the circle. Ask each child to try to choose an item that has not already been covered, but say that they may do so if they do not know the names of any of the items that have not been chosen earlier.

Support and extension

With younger children, name each item before playing the game. With older children, use items or pictures related to a theme you are exploring at the moment, such as minibeasts or dinosaurs.

Further ideas

■ When each child has chosen an item that they can name, ask them to say something special about it to the next child. For example, 'Can you cover a teapot? My granny has a gold one'.
■ Ask each child to say just the sound that their chosen item begins with, and not to name it until the next child has tried to cover it.
■ Encourage each child to make up a riddle, for example, 'Can you cover something that we use to paint with?'.

LEARNING OBJECTIVES

STEPPING STONE
Use vocabulary focused on objects and people who are of particular importance to them.

EARLY LEARNING GOAL
Extend their vocabulary, exploring the meanings and sounds of new words.

GROUP SIZE
Up to eight children.

HOME LINKS
Photocopy four or six related items on to a sheet of A4 paper, such as four or six different kinds of dinosaurs, minibeasts, fish or flowers. Let the children take them home to play 'Can you cover?' with their families.

Pandora says

What you need
Just the children.

What to do
This is a version of the game 'Simon says...'. Stand the children in a circle and choose one child to be 'Pandora' or 'Pandolpho' and to stand in the centre of the circle. Ask the child to say, 'Pandora (or Pandolpho) says "please put your hands on your heads"'. Explain that everyone in the circle must do what the 'Pandora' says, but only if 'Pandora' has remembered to say 'please'. Any child who is 'out' should sit at the side of the circle and help you to watch for other children who may be 'out'. Swap the child in the centre when they have had two or three turns.

Support and extension
Prepare younger children for their role as 'Pandora' or 'Pandolpho' by asking everyone to repeat action words together, making the appropriate movements such as pat, tickle, rub, nod, shake and clap. With older children, when one centre child finishes their two or three 'turns', ask them to choose another 'Pandora' or 'Pandolpho' by saying, 'Please..., come and be "Pandora" (or "Pandolpho")'.

Further ideas
■ Give the child in the centre of the circle a tambourine or sleigh bells, and ask them to shake them each time they remember to say 'please'.
■ Write the word 'please' on a piece of paper and attach to the front of a hat with sticky tape. The child in the centre of the circle should put on the hat each time they remember to say 'please'.
■ Play a version of 'Please, Mr Crocodile'. Choose a child from the circle to say to the centre child, 'Please, "Pandora" ("Pandolpho"), may I cross your river?' The centre child replies, 'Yes, you may cross my river, but only if you are wearing... (a certain colour or item of clothing)'.
■ Learn the word for 'please' in other languages and use it in your game.

LEARNING OBJECTIVES
STEPPING STONE
Use a widening range of words to express or elaborate ideas.

EARLY LEARNING GOAL
Speak clearly and audibly with confidence and control and show awareness of the listener, for example by their use of conventions such as greetings, 'please' and 'thank you'.

GROUP SIZE
Whole group.

HOME LINKS
Ask each child to make a very simple 'Pandora' or 'Pandolpho' finger puppet, using a tube of paper. Let each child take it home to play 'Pandora (Pandolpho) says'.

Communication, language and literacy

If...

What you need
The 'Can you guess?' photocopiable sheet on page 72; scissors; carpet square; shoe box with lid.

Preparation
Cut out the pictures on the sheet and put them inside the shoe box.

What to do
Stand together in a circle and place the carpet square next to one child. Explain that, when we start to do something, it is often a good idea to think about why we are doing it, and what might happen if we don't do it. To demonstrate, ask everyone to hold hands and move around while singing the following song, to the tune of 'If You're Happy and You Know it' (Traditional):

If you brush your teeth every day-ay
If you brush your teeth every day-ay
Your teeth will be alright
They'll be strong, clean and bright
But if you don't – then they won't!

So remember this important little rhyme
And try to think about it every time
And when you do a job
Always stop and think about
What might happen in the end if you don't!

At the end of the song, ask the child who is standing on the carpet square to take a picture from the box. Encourage them to talk about it and the 'consequence' beginning with 'If'. For example, 'If you go out in the snow in summer clothes, you will catch a cold!'. Remove the picture and continue the game.

Support and extension
With younger children, talk about each picture before the game. Ask older children to talk about any family anecdotes related to the pictures.

Further ideas
■ Put a comb, bar of soap, towel, toothbrush, empty shampoo bottle and scissors wrapped in cling film in the box. Ask everyone to say, 'If you don't use...'.
■ Enlarge the photocopiable sheet and cut out the picture of the boy watering the seeds. Fold a sheet of A4 paper in half and stick the picture on the front. Encourage the children to draw the 'consequence' of the picture on the inside, so that the top flap can be lifted to reveal it.

Mathematical development

The activities in this chapter help children to willingly attempt to count up to 10 objects, represent numbers using fingers and pictures and begin to understand subtraction and addition using the relevant terms, talk about, recognise and recreate simple patterns and use words to describe position.

Leg count

What you need
A hat.

What to do
Sit five children in a circle on the floor and ask the remaining child to stand in the centre. Invite one seated child to wear the hat to indicate the start of the circle. Ask everyone to stretch their legs in front of them. Say that if you lightly touch a child on the head they must 'hide' one leg by bending a knee and tucking their foot underneath their outstretched leg. Explain that you might ask them to hide two legs by sitting cross-legged. Walk around the outside of the circle, touching the heads of a few children and asking them to 'hide' one or both legs. Ask the child in the middle of the circle to count the remaining legs in the 'leg circle' one at a time.

Support and extension
Let younger children stretch out their arms instead of their legs. Ask them to 'hide' one or both arms behind their backs. With older children, say a number (up to ten) to the standing child and ask them to 'arrange' everyone's legs to show that number. So, for example, the child must say, '(Child's name), please tuck one leg away. (Child's name), please sit cross-legged'.

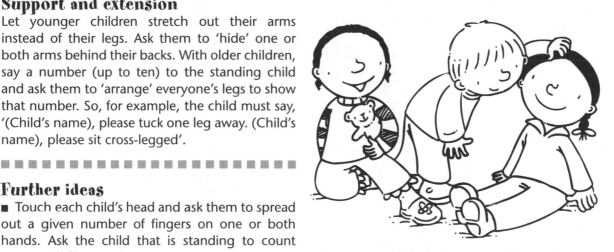

Further ideas
■ Touch each child's head and ask them to spread out a given number of fingers on one or both hands. Ask the child that is standing to count everyone's fingers.
■ Play 'Show me', with all six children sitting in the circle. Hold up cards showing a numeral 1, 2 or 0. Say, 'Show me one (two or zero) legs'.
■ Ask everyone to sit close together in a circle. Say, 'Let's make a circle using our legs', and tell the children to show one or two legs to make the circle. Count the number of legs out loud that you can see. Now, ask everyone to keep their legs in the same position, but to shuffle outwards and backwards to make a larger circle. Count the number of legs again, to show that the number is still the same whether they are 'squashed together' or 'spread out'.

LEARNING OBJECTIVES
STEPPING STONE
Willingly attempt to count, with some numbers in the correct order.

EARLY LEARNING GOAL
Count reliably up to 10 everyday objects.

GROUP SIZE
Six children.

HOME LINKS
Ask children to count the legs of everyone in their family, and to tell you how many there are.

Secret numbers

LEARNING OBJECTIVES
STEPPING STONE
Begin to represent numbers using fingers, marks on paper or pictures.

EARLY LEARNING GOAL
Recognise numerals 1 to 9.

GROUP SIZE
Up to ten children.

What you need
A set of numerals 1 to 9.

What to do
Sit together on the floor in a circle and invite one child to leave the circle. Show this child the set of numerals and ask them to point to one. Hold up the numeral and encourage the child to trace on top of it, and then on your palm with their finger. Invite the child to rejoin the circle, but not to tell anyone which number they chose.

Now encourage that child to whisper the number in the ear of the person next to them and to trace it on that person's palm. Then invite that child to whisper the number to the child next to them and to trace it on their palm, and so on. The last child to 'receive' the whispered and traced number should say it out loud. Ask the first child whether or not their chosen number has 'travelled' accurately around the circle.

Support and extension
With younger children, reduce the number of children in the circle and limit the numerals shown to two or three at a time. Write these on a piece of A4 paper for each child to place on the floor in front of them, and to pass on to the next child. When playing with older children, ask them to close their eyes so they cannot see the 'tracer' tracing the number. Some older children may be able to play without a set of numerals. Ask the 'chooser' to whisper their number to you at the start of each round.

Further ideas
■ Encourage the children to use a small paintbrush, toothbrush or straw to trace the numbers on their palms, instead of their fingers.
■ Let individual children draw a 'secret' number, using a yellow or white crayon, on half a piece of A4 paper. Remind them to apply pressure. Let another child paint over it with a thin wash of paint to reveal the number.
■ Using the blunt end of a ballpoint pen, invite individual children to draw a number on paper with lemon juice. When dry, let another child shine a torch behind the paper to reveal the number.

HOME LINKS
Ask the children to say to a family member, 'Close your eyes and guess which number I'm writing on your hand'.

Teddies united!

What you need
Eleven copies of the 'Teddy's team' photocopiable sheet on page 74; scissors; felt-tipped pens; sticky tape on a dispenser; eleven teddy bears; medium-sized plastic ball.

Preparation
Cut out each 'shirt' on the photocopiable sheets and write a numeral on each one, from 1 to 11. Colour the stripes. Some or all of the cutting, writing numerals and colouring may be done by the children.

What to do
Sit the children on the floor in a semi-circle, and give each child a teddy bear. Sit yourself and a colleague on the floor facing the children. Explain that you are the 'football team manager', your colleague is the 'trainer' and that the bears are 'players'. Say that the 'players' are each going to have a new 'strip' (shirt) with a number on it. Call out a number to each child in order from 1 to 11. Check that they can remember 'their' number. Tell the children that, when you hold up each shirt, they must look at the number on the front. If it is their number, they should come and collect the shirt.

Hold up the shirts in random order. As each child comes forward, ask your 'trainer' to stick the shirt on the front of each bear with two pieces of sticky tape. When all the bears are wearing their shirts, ask your 'trainer' to call out a number and roll the ball to the bear. The child holding the bear can help it to kick the ball back to the 'trainer'.

Support and extension
Call out younger children to receive their shirts in numerical order. Before each older child is called, ask your 'trainer' to hold up the relevant number of fingers for each bear to count, before holding up each shirt.

Further ideas
■ Ask everyone to try putting the bears in order in a circle for a team 'huddle'.
■ Make a display of replica football shirts or use magazine photographs and posters. Discuss the numbers.
■ Photocopy the sheet 11 times. Colour and number the shirts from 1 to 11. Stick each sheet on a piece of A4 card, cover in film, punch two holes at the top and thread with wool. Let a team of children wear them outside for simple ball-kicking games.

The hungry duck

What you need
One plastic duck (preferably with a squeak); piece of string, approximately 50cm long; ten white plastic counting cubes; tray; chairs.

Preparation
Tie the string around the duck so that it may be pulled along. Put the cubes on the tray.

What to do
Gather the children together in a circle, sitting on chairs, and explain that they are sitting around a 'duck pond'. Show them the duck and the cubes, and explain that the duck loves to eat 'cubes of bread'. Tell the children that everyone can take turns to make the duck 'swim' by pulling the string, and they can also feed the duck the 'bread cubes'. Give the duck to one child and ask them to pull it sideways and then pass it on to the next child. As the children make the duck swim, sing the following song with them, to the tune of 'Five little ducks went swimming one day' (Traditional). When the children have sung up to the end of the third line, ask them to sing the name of the child holding the string at that point. Ask the child to keep the string and not 'pass it on':

One hungry duck went swimming one day
Round the pond, all the way.
When it got to... (child's name)
It stopped, and this is what... said:

Ask the child to say, 'How many cubes of bread would you like?'. Ask the child standing next to the child holding the string, to 'squeak' the duck a number of times (any number up to ten) or to say 'quack' a number of times. The child holding the string then counts out the right number of cubes from the tray for the duck.

Support and extension
With younger children use only five cubes. Ask older children to count out cubes to place on the 'Count the quacks!' photocopiable sheet on page 75.

Further ideas
■ Instead of squeaking the duck or saying 'quack', ask a child to scrape the ridged 'grip' panel on the side of an empty washing-up liquid bottle with a lollipop stick.
■ Use pipe-cleaner worms instead of bread cubes.
■ Let one child be the duck, wearing a yellow hat.

Magic circles

What you need
One adult-sized chair; one shop-bought or home-made 'magic wand'.

What to do
Ask everyone to sit on the floor in a circle. Place an adult-sized chair between two of the children. Invite four children to stand in the centre, holding hands in a small circle. Ask another child to be a 'magician', who sits on the chair with the wand. Say that the magician can use the wand to change the size of the circle of children from a small circle, to a middle-sized circle and then to a large circle.

Encourage the magician to say, 'Abracadabra! Please make a small circle!'. The children in the centre should huddle together to make the smallest circle they can. Ask everybody to count how many children there are in the small circle. Now encourage the magician to magic a middle-sized circle and then a large circle. Ask the children if there are more or less in each circle and prompt them to notice that there are always only four children. Ask the magician to reduce the large circle to a middle-sized circle, and then to a small one.

Support and extension
With younger children ask the magician to only make big and little circles. With older children, ask the four children in the centre to stand side-by-side in a line, holding hands. The magician should magic a short, medium-sized and long line. Ask everyone to count and say how many children are in the line each time.

Further ideas
■ Invite three children to be 'The Three Bears', holding hands in the centre and wearing bear 'ears', if available.
■ Ask five children to be speckled frogs standing in a row in the centre, each child wearing a green crêpe paper cape on which are drawn black speckles.

The busy farmer

What you need
Six plastic eggs or six egg shapes cut from cardboard; a shopping basket; a shoe box.

What to do
Sit everyone on the floor in a circle. Explain that the space in the middle is a farm with a fence all around it. Ask one child to be the farmer, who stands at one side of the centre space in the 'cowshed'. Ask another child to be a hen, who kneels at the other side in the 'hen coop'. Place the eggs in a shoebox and position them behind the hen.

Explain that every morning, while the farmer was milking the cow, the hen would start clucking and lay some eggs. Say that the farmer would stop milking, walk all the way to the coop, collect the eggs in the basket and say, 'Thank you!'. Say the farmer would walk all the way back to the cowshed, but then the hen would always start clucking again and lay some more eggs so that the farmer would have to go back all over again! Say, for example, 'The farmer collected two eggs first of all, then another one. How many eggs is that altogether?'. Repeat with different pairs of children and different numbers of eggs.

Support and extension
Use only four eggs with younger children. Give older children pretending to be the farmer a six-egg carton to fill instead of a basket. Challenge the 'hen' to lay six eggs altogether every time, in two batches.

Further ideas
■ Ask six children to curl up like chicks, side-by-side behind the hen. The farmer can be surprised each morning to collect two batches of newly-hatched chicks!
■ Instead of a hen, encourage one child to be the farm cat who produces two litters of kittens (the children can be curled up).
■ Lay six carrots in a corner of the centre space. Ask a farmer to pretend to dig up some, put them in the basket, return to the cowshed and then remember that there are more carrots to be dug.

Balloon bounce

What you need
A small tablecloth or short curtain; four balloons in the same colour. Remember never to leave children unattended when playing with balloons.

What to do
Ask everyone to stand in a circle, holding the tablecloth or curtain between them. Place the balloons on the material and encourage everyone to count them. Ask the children to start gently shaking the material. Challenge them to try to make some, but not all, of the balloons fall off. When one or more balloons have fallen off, ask the children to count how many balloons are left. Replace the fallen balloon(s) each time and repeat the game.

Support and extension
With younger children, tie a short piece of string to each balloon. Ask everyone to hold the material very still so that no balloons fall off. Invite the children to count the balloons and say how many would be left if one fell off. Using the strings, pull one balloon away, then ask the children to predict how many would be left on each occasion, and then check the results. For the older children, have up to six balloons. Say, 'We have six balloons. If all six balloons fell off, how many would be left?'. Ask the children to 'bounce off' all the balloons and answer, 'None, nought or zero'.

Further ideas
■ Play 'Bouncing bears on the bed', using teddy bears on the tablecloth or curtain.
■ Play the game outside, using a parachute and light-weight balls.
■ Ask the children to make a small circle, so that the material sags, to create a 'nest'. Tie string on each balloon and draw eyes, a beak and wings with a felt-tipped pen to transform them into fledglings in a nest. Ask everyone to count them. Now, invite the children to blow, sounding like a windy day, and to shake the nest gently. Say that the fledglings decide to fly away, as you gently pull one or more balloons upwards and ask how many are left.

LEARNING OBJECTIVES
STEPPING STONE
Show an interest in number problems.

EARLY LEARNING GOAL
Begin to relate addition to combining two groups of objects and subtraction to 'taking away'.

GROUP SIZE
Six children.

HOME LINKS
Let everyone roll up four small silver foil balls (to take home in an envelope), and place carefully on a wooden spoon. Ask everyone to walk with it, or shake it gently, counting how many balls are left each time some fall.

33

The giant's necklace

What you need
A tray of threading beads or cubes in three colours; a piece of wool, approximately 3m long; sticky tape; drawstring bag; chairs.

Preparation
Tie a large knot at one end of the wool. Roll a small piece of sticky tape around the other end to make it easy to thread through the beads. Put one bead of each colour in the bag.

What to do
Sit the children on chairs in a circle. Explain that you would like everyone to help you make a giant's necklace, using beads or cubes in a pattern of three colours. Invite three of the children to each choose a bead from the bag. Hold up the beads and say, 'Let's try to make the necklace using a pattern in the colours of these beads' (for example, red, green, yellow). Ask everyone to repeat the names of the colours, in order.

Put the tray of beads on the floor in the centre of the circle. Place the string in a circle on the children's laps, with the knotted end on one child's lap and another child holding the taped threading end. Encourage this child to say out loud the sequence of three colours, before picking the appropriate beads from the tray. Invite the child to thread them and to pass the threading end of the wool to the next child. Ask this child to say out loud the three colours of the pattern in the correct order, to pick the beads from the tray and then thread them. Encourage the children to pass on the wool until everyone has had a turn.

Support and extension
Use only two colours of bead with younger children. Extend to four colours with older children.

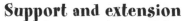

Further ideas
■ Make a large wall display of a collaged giant wearing his colourful necklace!

■ Wash some green and black grapes. Give each child a thin plastic straw, and ask them to 'thread' four grapes in alternate colours, to make a grape 'kebab'.

■ Enjoy making patterned 'kebabs' for a teddy bears' picnic by threading play dough or Plasticine on to thin plastic straws.

LEARNING OBJECTIVES

STEPPING STONE
Show interest by sustained construction activity or by talking about shapes or arrangements.

EARLY LEARNING GOAL
Talk about, recognise and recreate simple patterns.

GROUP SIZE
Six children.

HOME LINKS
Let the children make necklaces or bracelets using different-coloured pasta to take home.

The lost baby

What you need
A 'woodland' soft toy, such as a squirrel or hedgehog; drum; sleigh bells.

What to do
Stand all but one child in a circle, with plenty of space between them. Encourage the children to spread their arms and to pretend they are trees in a forest. Stand one child a short distance away from the forest, facing away from the trees. Explain that this child is the mother or father of the woodland animal. While the 'parent' has their back to the forest, hide the soft toy baby on one of the trees by, for example, tucking it under a child's jumper.

Encourage the parent to run in and out of the trees, looking for their 'baby'. Tell the parent that if you play a drum, they must stop in front of the nearest tree. If you play sleigh bells they must stop behind the tree. When the child stops, ask them to say where they are, for example, 'I am standing behind a tree'. The child should then gently inspect the tree to see if the baby is hidden there. If it is, the parent receives a round of applause and changes places with the tree, who becomes the next parent. If the baby is not in the searched tree, the two children still change places, and the game continues until the baby is found.

Support and extension
Do not use the percussion instruments with younger children. Instead, give oral instructions, for example, 'Please stand in front of a tree'. With older children, add the phrase 'next to' or 'by the side of', accompanied by a third instrument such as woodblocks.

Further ideas
■ At times when the children queue up throughout the day, ask them to say where they are, for example, 'I am behind Rashid and in front of Emma'.
■ Make toy car traffic jams and invite the children to describe the position of particular vehicles.

Mathematical development

Bear's busy day

What you need
One teddy bear; a plastic or wooden cube, cuboid and cylinder; ball; paper cone; tray.

What to do
Sit everyone on the floor in a circle and put the items on the tray in the centre. Hold up the bear and explain that you are going to tell a story called 'Bear's busy day' (see below). After each section, say to a different child, 'Do you know the name of the shape? Can you point to it and hold it up for us to see?'.
- For breakfast, Bear shook his favourite cereal from a big box. It had six sides and each side was a rectangle. (Cuboid.)
- Then Bear went out to play football. The ball was round all over. (Sphere.)
- After lunch, Bear put a scoop of ice-cream on top of something crunchy. It had a round wide top, and a point at the bottom. (Cone.)
- Then Bear was very happy to find one of his building blocks under the table. The block had six sides and every side was a square shape. (Cube.)
- In the afternoon, Bear made an apple pie. He used his new rolling pin to roll the dough. It was round at both ends and its sides were curved. (Cylinder.)

Support and extension
With younger children, hold up the shapes before the game and name them. With older children, put the shapes in a drawstring bag. Pass it around the circle and let each child close their eyes, take out a shape, describe how it feels and try to name it.

Further ideas
- Play 'Solid shape I spy'. Put objects, such as a dice, tissue box, washing-up liquid bottle, orange and a cone-shaped party hat on a table. Let each child say, 'I spy, with my little eye, something on this table which is a cylinder shape.'
- Introduce different names of solid shapes into well-known fairy stories. For example, 'Goldilocks first tried Daddy bear's bed, but the mattress, which was a cuboid shape, was too hard.'

Knowledge and understanding of the world

The activities in this chapter will encourage the children to describe simple features of objects and events, show an awareness of change, ask questions, use a computer to complete a simple program and identify the right tools for a task.

Spider's web

What you need
A toy spider; a ball of thick wool with two loose ends; a tambourine.

What to do
Sit everyone on the floor in a circle with plenty of space in between each child. Hold up a toy spider and invite the children to tell you what they know about them. Talk about the number of legs and eyes of most spiders (eight), favourite food (insects such as moths and flies), how they catch insects (by spinning webs), how they walk on walls and ceilings (using special pads on their feet), and the name of baby spiders (spiderlings).

Invite one child to be a spider and give them the ball of wool to hold. Say that everyone else is a twig on a tree and the spider is going to weave a web between them. Ask the children to stand up and invite the spider to give one end of wool to one of the 'twigs' to hold. As you shake the tambourine, the spider should spin a web by unwinding the wool as they touch each child in the circle, in any order, and giving each child the wool to hold at that point. Explain that it does not matter if a twig is visited twice, but ask the spider to try to touch every child at least once. When the web is spun, ask the spider to stand still for 'spider question time' and let the rest of the children ask questions about what it is like being a spider.

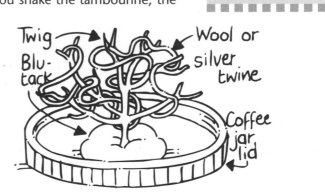

Support and extension
With younger children, call out the names of the twigs that the spider needs to touch and omit the spider question time. Ask older children to stand in two circles, one inside the other.

Further ideas
■ Secure a small twig in a lump of Blu-Tack and let individual children spin webs with wool or silver twine (see illustration above).
■ Spin colourful webs on peg-boards by threading wool around pegs.

LEARNING OBJECTIVES
STEPPING STONE
Show an interest in why things happen and how things work.

EARLY LEARNING GOAL
Ask questions about why things happen and how things work.

GROUP SIZE
Up to eight children.

HOME LINKS
Ask families to help their children look for webs in and around the house and garden.

Are you my baby?

LEARNING OBJECTIVES
STEPPING STONE
Show curiosity and interest by facial expression, movement or sound.

EARLY LEARNING GOAL
Find out about, and identify, some features of living things, objects and events they observe.

GROUP SIZE
Up to seven children.

What you need
A table; curtain or sheet; chairs.

What to do
Arrange six chairs in a semi-circle around a table. Cover the table with the curtain or sheet. Invite the children to sit on the chairs and explain that the table is a cave. Invite one child to crawl into the cave and tell them that they are a baby farm animal playing 'Hide and seek' with its parent. Ask the baby to decide which animal they are pretending to be, but not to tell anyone! Ask the remaining children to be different parent animals who make special sounds, for example, a sheep, pig, horse, hen, duck or cow.

Invite each child in turn to kneel next to the cave and say, for example, 'Baa, baa, are you my baby?'. The baby answers, 'You are a sheep, and I think you are really… (name of child), and I am not your baby!' until they choose to answer, 'Baa, baa, yes I am your baby!'.

Support and extension
Do not ask younger children to guess the names of the children pretending to be the parent animals. With older children, talk about how sheep bleat, pigs grunt, horses whinny or neigh, hens cluck, ducks quack and cows moo. When each baby has recognised the parent animal's sound and tried to identify the child, ask the baby, 'Does a sheep bleat or grunt?', and so on.

HOME LINKS
Let the children make four card stand-up farm animals each (see illustration), to take home to play 'Kim's game'. To play, the child looks at the cards and turns around while a partner hides one card. The child turns around again and says which animal is missing. If they are correct, the partner produces the card and makes the appropriate sound.

Further ideas
■ When each baby has said, 'I am your baby!' ask them to say what baby animal they are, for example, 'I am a lamb'.
■ Let the children pretend to be wild animals such as baby snakes, monkeys, lions, tigers, hyenas and crocodiles, and recognise the sounds that their parents make.
■ Ask the children to pretend to be different kinds of baby birds, such as woodpeckers, cuckoos, parrots, pigeons and owls, and recognise the sounds that their parents make.

Silky story

What you need
Nine copies of the 'Silkworm song' photocopiable sheet on page 76; pair of scissors; eight clipboards; one silk item (if possible); one reel of yellow polyester sewing thread.

Preparation
Cut out the pictures from one photocopiable sheet. Clip the remaining sheets to the clipboards.

What to do
Sit everyone in a circle on the floor. Hold up the silk item (if available) and pass it around, asking the children to describe how it feels. Tell the children that it is made from silk, a material made by silkworms, which are a kind of caterpillar. Pass around each picture one at a time, with a simple explanation of each one. For example, the baby silkworm hatches from a tiny egg. It eats lots of leaves from a mulberry bush or lettuce leaves. It keeps growing and splits and changes its skin four times. Then it spins a cocoon of long, yellowy silk thread which people use to make clothes. (Pass around the reel of thread.) Then it changes into a chrysalis and eventually hatches into a moth.

Give everyone a clipboard and sheet for a quick recap, asking, 'What happens next?'. Collect the clipboards and ask everyone to lie on their tummy and pretend to be a silkworm. Sing the song on the sheet with the children, inviting their suggestions for movements.

Support and extension
With younger children, say a sentence about each picture but leave out the final word for the children to supply. For example, 'The silkworm spins a...'. With older children, relate the silkworm life-cycle to that of a caterpillar changing into a butterfly. You can adapt the song by changing the word 'silkworms' to 'caterpillars', 'mulberry bush' to 'cabbage', 'moth' to 'butterfly', and the third verse to:

> Now we change into a chrysalis
> Into a chrysalis, into a chrysalis.
> Now we change into a chrysalis
> Yes, we do!

Further ideas
■ Share the book *Life Cycle of a Silkworm* (Heinemann) and encourage the children to recount the sequence.
■ Set up a real silkworm farm. Details are available on www.silkworm-supplies.co.uk.
■ Cut up the pictures on the photocopiable sheet and muddle them up. Let pairs of children put them in the correct order.

Round and round the circus

What you need
A programmable floor toy such as Roamer or Turtle; a doll dressed as a clown; masking tape.

Preparation
Sit the doll on the programmable toy and secure with masking tape.

What to do
Sit everyone in a circle on the floor and explain that you are going to pretend that you are at the circus. Show the children the clown doll sitting on the programmable toy and ask them to suggest a name for the clown. Explain that the clown has a new electronic vehicle to travel around the circus ring. Tell the children that they can program the vehicle to make the clown visit other children, so that it can say, 'Hello'. Ask for a volunteer programmer and help the child to program the toy to stop at another child of their choice. Ask the programmer to pretend to be the clown saying, 'Hello' to the chosen child. That child should say, 'Hello… (name of programmer)', and have a go at programming the toy to visit another child in the circle.

Support and extension
With younger children, ask the child who has been chosen by the programmer to sit directly opposite the programmer in the circle. Older children could take it in turns to instruct another child in carrying out the necessary steps to control the vehicle and program it towards someone else.

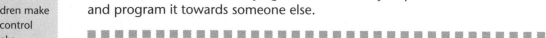

Further ideas
■ Remove the clown's hat. Place it on the floor in the centre space and ask for volunteers to program the toy to travel to the lost hat. Ask the programmer to replace the hat on the clown's head.
■ Transform the programmable toy into a frog, travelling between lily pads in a pond, looking for grubs.
■ Decorate the programmable toy to look like a submarine. Program it to travel along the seabed in order to locate a shipwreck.

Busy bees

What you need
Four kinds of artificial summer flowers (two of each), such as sunflowers, daisies, poppies and roses; one chair, covered with a piece of brown fabric.

What to do
Sit eight children in a circle, spaced well apart. Leave a large space in the circle for the 'beehive' (the chair covered in brown fabric). Explain that inside the circle is a summer flower garden. Hold up and name each of the flowers, and

then give one flower to eight of the children. Ask the remaining child to be a bee. Talk about how bees collect nectar from the flowers which they take back to the beehive and make into honey.

Say that you are going to play a game. Explain that on each outing, a bee will collect nectar from only one kind of flower. Ask the bee to stand in front of the beehive and fly between the flowers, pretending to lap up nectar from two matching flowers before returning to the beehive. Before the bee starts flying, ask which kind of flower they will be visiting. As the bee flies, ask everyone to sing the song below, to the tune of 'Old Macdonald Had a Farm' (Traditional):

> *... (name of child) Bee is buzzing round*
> *E-I-E-I buzz!*
> *Buzzing here and buzzing there*
> *E-I-E-I buzz!*

Support and extension
Younger children can just visit two of the same type of flower, without naming them. With older children, write the flower names on pieces of A4 paper for everyone to hold instead of flowers. Ask the bee to read the names, looking carefully at the initial letters.

Further ideas
■ Tell the children that a bee carries out a special dance that tells the other bees to follow it to some nectar. Ask two 'bees' to stand in front of the beehive. Encourage one to make up a bee dance and then to visit one of the flowers. The second bee should see which flower the first bee visited, and find a matching one to visit.
■ Explain that some bees are worker bees; they clean and repair the hive, make honey and feed the young bees. Let the children make up appropriate actions for the different jobs that the worker bees do.

LEARNING OBJECTIVES
STEPPING STONE
Describe simple features of objects and events.

EARLY LEARNING GOAL
Find out about, and identify, some features of living things, objects and events they observe.

GROUP SIZE
Nine children.

HOME LINKS
Let the children prepare and take home a honey sandwich to talk about and share.

Come in from the rain

What you need
A large golf umbrella; a large waste bin; three large curtains.

Preparation
Open up the umbrella and stand it in the waste bin. Secure it by packing the curtains around the handle so the umbrella stands upright.

What to do
Sit everyone on the floor in a circle. Ask the children why people use umbrellas. Discuss the fact that people need umbrellas to keep them dry in the rain, but some animals have special coverings that keep them dry. Talk about fur, feathers, wool and hide. Invite everyone to choose to be a particular animal, or themselves. Ask one child to sit under the umbrella and another to gently drum their fingertips on top of the umbrella, to sound like raindrops.

   Invite the seated child to choose someone in the circle and say, 'Would you like to shelter under my umbrella?'. If the child they have chosen is pretending to be him or herself, they must answer, 'Yes, please', and change places. Choose a new rainmaker. If the child being asked to shelter is pretending to be an animal, they must answer, 'No, thank you. I am a duck'. Ask them to become the new rainmaker and choose another child to sit under the umbrella.

Support and extension
Help younger children to decide what to be by holding up a tray of plastic animals. Ask older children to add a sentence describing their covering. For example, 'I am a sheep and I have a woolly coat to protect me' or, 'I am Alex and I have my raincoat and Wellingtons to protect me'.

Further ideas
■ Make a book of drawings about animals and their coverings that keep them dry.

■ Put a stone, a piece of paper, a thin slice of apple, a dead leaf and a sturdy plant growing in a pot, on a tray. Ask everyone to predict what will happen to each item if it is left out in the rain. On a rainy day, place the tray outside. When you bring it back in, discuss what has happened. Talk about the items that have not been affected by the rain (the stone and the pot plant). What has happened to the other items?

Sensory circle

What you need
Five pieces of A4 card in different colours; felt-tipped pens; a variety of interesting natural or manufactured objects (up to four at a time).

Preparation
Copy the designs (see illustration below) on to the coloured card to make 'senses cards'. Check for food allergies to any of the edible objects in your collection.

What to do
Ask the children to wash their hands, then gather everyone together in a circle on the floor. Hold up and talk about each card, inviting the children to suggest which sense is shown on each card. Choose one item to investigate – perhaps an edible item such as an aubergine, courgette or star fruit. Spread out all or some of the cards in the centre of the circle, depending on which senses are appropriate for the investigation of a particular item. (For objects that you do not want the children to taste, omit the 'taste' sense card.) Pass the object around the circle. Say the name of the item and ask everyone to think about what it looks and feels like and, if appropriate, what it smells, sounds and tastes like.

Remind everyone that they must never put anything in their mouths without first asking an adult whether it is safe to do so. After the item has been passed around the circle, invite one child to select a sense card and say, for example, 'This aubergine looks like a dark pear'. Continue with the other cards, encouraging the children to be as descriptive as possible about all of the items.

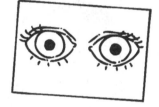
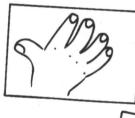

Support and extension
With younger children, put only one card at a time in the centre of the circle. Jot down the different comments from older children to make into a riddle book.

Further ideas
■ If you are using edible items that cannot be tasted during circle time, arrange for them to be used in simple recipes to be eaten later.
■ Show an item to one child. Let everyone else ask 'sense' questions, for example, 'What does it feel like?', to try to work out what it is.

Family helpers

What you need

Six copies of the 'Can we help?' photocopiable sheet on page 77; six clipboards; table; toy landline telephone; toy mobile telephone; notepad; pencil; chairs.

Preparation

Arrange seven chairs in a semi-circle. At the open end of the semi-circle, position the table and place your chair behind it so that you are facing the children. Put the landline telephone, notepad and pencil on the table. Attach the photocopiable sheets to the clipboards.

What to do

Give each child a clipboard and encourage everyone to talk about occasions when they may have encountered any of the people and situations illustrated. Explain that when somebody needs a washing machine repair person, a dentist or car mechanic, they need to telephone first (perhaps using a mobile telephone for a car breakdown). Before people visit the Post Office, the library or a shop, they sometimes telephone first to find out when it is open.

Ask for a volunteer to pretend to be someone who needs to telephone a family helper. Give the child the toy mobile telephone and ask them who they would like to ring. Play the role of the helper yourself, sitting behind the table. Conduct a conversation in which the child explains why they are ringing and gives you any other important details. Let everyone see you jotting down the details on your note pad. Act out a response to the child's call for help.

Support and extension

With younger children, let each child be the helper while you use the telephone to call them. Let pairs of older children conduct a conversation, one as helper and one telephoning for help.

Further ideas

■ Look through a copy of the Yellow Pages together. Explain that this is where we can find the numbers of lots of people that can help us.
■ Encourage the children to suggest other reasons for making telephone calls, such as inviting a friend to play or ringing to say 'hello' to granny.

Fix it!

What you need
Furnished dolls' house; table; chairs.

Preparation
Arrange eight chairs in a semi-circle. At the open end of the semi-circle, arrange the table with a chair behind it facing the children. Put the dolls' house on the table, to the side of the chair.

What to do
Invite everyone to sit on a chair. Explain that all houses need to be repaired sometimes, so that people can be comfortable and safe. Talk about the names of the rooms in a house and hold up and describe items of furniture from the dolls' house. Ask everyone to think about any repairs that might need carrying out in a living room, considering items of furniture, objects in the living room, repairs to the walls, windows, ceilings and floor.

Invite one volunteer at a time to sit on the chair next to the dolls' house. Encourage the child to talk about a particular repair, holding up any items of furniture, if necessary. Ask the child to describe the problem and to talk about how it could be remedied. For example, 'The leg could break off this chair and make it dangerous. You could fix it with a hammer and nails, or glue it back together' or 'If there was a hole in a cushion on your sofa, some feathers might come out. You could use a needle and cotton to sew it up again'. Continue discussing potential repairs to all the rooms in the house.

Support and extension
With younger children, instead of talking about repairs, talk about what might need cleaning in each room and what would be required. With older children, talk about repairs outside the house, such as a leaking roof, broken window or jobs in the garden.

Further ideas
■ Let individual children cut out a picture of a do-it-yourself item from a catalogue, stick it on to paper and draw themselves alongside, as if they are using it. Stress the importance of wearing safety clothing such as goggles, gloves and overalls.
■ Make a list of the names and telephone numbers of repair people used by your setting, so children can telephone them in home-corner role-play.

LEARNING OBJECTIVES
STEPPING STONE
Realise tools can be used for a purpose.

EARLY LEARNING GOAL
Select the tools and techniques they need to shape, assemble and join materials they are using.

GROUP SIZE
Up to eight children.

HOME LINKS
Ask children to find out about repairs that have been carried out at home. Encourage them to share their findings with the group.

Teddy's lost key

What you need
Six copies of the 'Teddy's journey' photocopiable sheet on page 78; six clipboards; one small-world item to represent each picture, for example, a bridge, a slide, a building, a garage, a train station and a flower; a key; a small teddy bear.

Preparation
Attach the photocopiable sheets to the clipboards.

What to do
Sit everybody on chairs in a circle and give each child a clipboard and sheet. Hold up the bear and explain that he has lost his key. Tell the children that he has looked everywhere, but he can't find it. Ask everyone to point to each picture, as you mention each location where Teddy has searched. At the end of the story, hold up the flower, to represent Teddy's garden, and the key.

Now give out the six small-world items to the children, making sure they are in the same order as the locations on the photocopiable sheet. Give the teddy and the key to the last child in the circle, who should be holding the flower. Sing the song on the sheet together and encourage the children to pass the bear around the circle, holding up the bear and their small-world item when the words apply to them.

Support and extension
Before singing the song with younger children, hold up the bear and each small-world feature. Say, 'Where is the bear now?'. With older children, put the small-world items on the floor in the centre of the circle. Let everyone choose their own, in random order, but ensure that the flower remains the last item. Ask everyone to sing the song, changing the order of the words accordingly.

Further ideas
■ Make up a song together involving other locations.
■ Let children walk the bear along a road mat printed with various town features. Ask the children to make up a song about the places he passes, looking for his key.

LEARNING OBJECTIVES
STEPPING STONE
Show an interset in the world in which they live.

EARLY LEARNING GOAL
Observe, find out about and identify features in the place they live and the natural world.

GROUP SIZE
Six children.

HOME LINKS
Let individual children take home a photocopiable sheet so that they can try to spot some of the locations when they are out with their families.

Physical development

This chapter suggests a range of ideas to help children move around with confidence, control and co-ordination, showing an awareness of space, for themselves and others, to recognise the importance of keeping healthy, retrieve, collect and catch objects and begin to use tools with one hand.

Horse moves

What you need
A hobbyhorse; an apple.

What to do
Stand together in a circle. Explain that, today, your circle is a showring at a horse show, and you are all going to watch the horses. Tell the children that horses can change speed when they move. Explain that, as well as walking, they can trot, canter and gallop. Hold up the hobbyhorse and tell the children that its name is 'Appledore'. Say that 'Appledore' loves to eat apples. Ask one child to ride 'Appledore' around the showring, while everyone sings the following song to the tune of 'This is the Way the Ladies Ride' (Traditional):

> Appledore – please walk, walk, walk,
> Trot, trot, trot,
> Canter, canter, canter.
> Appledore – please gallop, gallop, gallop
> Now please slow down and HALT!

Just before they sing the last line, give one child an apple to hold up in the air. Ask the rider to halt in front of the child holding the apple. This child should pretend to feed 'Appledore' and then swap places to be the next rider.

Support and extension
Younger children can focus on just one speed and sing the following version:

> This is the way Appledore trots,
> Appledore trots, Appledore trots.
> This is the way Appledore trots
> All the way round the showring.

With older children, place a few flat bricks in the space to represent jumps.

Further ideas
- Instead of using a hobbyhorse, ask pairs of children to be 'Appledore' and the rider. Let 'Appledore' wear a set of walking reins with bells on the front.
- Use the space as an athletics stadium. Ask children to be competitors who walk, jog, run, sprint and stop. Change the words of the song accordingly.

LEARNING OBJECTIVES
STEPPING STONE
Adjust speed or change direction to avoid obstacles.

EARLY LEARNING GOAL
Move with confidence, imagination and in safety.

GROUP SIZE
Whole group.

HOME LINKS
Invite the children to draw horses on pieces of folded card and stick them on to plastic aerosol lids with sticky tape. Let the children take them home and use them to tap on a surface to sound like a horse walking, trotting, cantering or galloping.

Humming circle

What you need
One piece of card, measuring 10cm by 10cm; felt-tipped pen; sticky tape.

Preparation
Draw a hummingbird on the card (see illustration below).

What to do
Sit ten children on chairs in a semi-circle. Ask five children to stand opposite them, and explain that they are going to be the trees. Hold up your picture of a hummingbird, and explain that it is called a hummingbird because it makes a humming sound by beating its wings together in a special way. Tell the children that hummingbirds can fly up, down, backwards, forwards, from side to side, and that they can hover.

Explain that the hummingbird you are holding is a baby bird who is hiding in a tree. Ask one seated child to be the parent bird who is looking for their baby. Encourage the child to stand with their back to the chairs and trees, then stick the baby bird on to the back of one of the 'trees' using sticky tape.

Ask the trees to spread their arms upwards and outwards, like branches. Invite the parent bird to pretend to fly backwards, forwards, sideways, up and down, looking for their baby. The seated children should help by humming loudly if the parent is flying close to the tree in which the baby is hiding, and humming quietly if the parent flies away from the tree.

Support and extension
Instead of humming, ask seated younger children to say 'yes' or 'no', to help the parent bird find the baby. With older children, ask each 'parent' to describe the direction in which they are flying.

Further ideas
■ Switch off the lights and draw the blinds. Give one child a torch and encourage them to pretend to follow the movements of a flying owl by moving the torch in different directions.

■ Let individual children fly a toy helicopter over a road mat in search of an injured play person. Encourage them to describe their movements, for example, 'I'm flying forwards, and now I'm hovering above the garage'.

LEARNING OBJECTIVES

STEPPING STONE
Go backwards and sideways as well as forwards.

EARLY LEARNING GOAL
Move with confidence, imagination and in safety.

GROUP SIZE
15 children.

HOME LINKS
Ask families to play mirroring games with their children. Encourage them to try to match each other in moving up, down, forwards, backwards and sideways.

Arctic circle

What you need
Eight carpet squares; cassette or CD player; medium-paced music.

What to do
Gather everyone standing together in a circle. Tell the children that you are going to pretend to be polar bears at the North Pole, where it is very cold. Explain that the carpet squares are ice floes that have broken off an iceberg, and arrange the ice floes at random intervals in the centre space. Tell the children that when polar bears jump from floe to floe, they never slip or lose their balance. This is because they have rough skin and hairs on their feet, which helps them to grip the ice.

Ask each 'bear' to stand on a floe. Tell the children that you are going to play the music, and when it starts, they should jump from floe to floe, trying not to fall into the water. Explain that, when the music stops, they must freeze and try to balance on whichever part of their body they may have landed on. If anyone moves when they are 'freezing', they can move to the side and help you to watch the others.

Support and extension
With younger children, simplify the game by reducing the number of players. Instead of music, use a tambourine and say, 'Freeze!'. With older children, remove one of the carpet squares each time and play the game in a similar way to 'Musical chairs'.

Further ideas
■ Fill the water tray with warm water and let children play with real ice floes made by freezing water in cottage cheese pots. Add some miniature polar bears to the tray.
■ Let children pretend to be penguins in Antarctica. Ask them to waddle and jump from floe to floe when the music begins.
■ Play the 'Wobble game'. Challenge children to balance on different parts of their bodies and to see which number they can count up to before beginning to wobble.

LEARNING OBJECTIVES
STEPPING STONE
Sit up, stand up and balance on various parts of the body.

EARLY LEARNING GOAL
Move with control and co-ordination.

GROUP SIZE
Eight children.

HOME LINKS
Encourage the children to explain how to play the 'Wobble game' to members of their family, and to play it at home. Invite the children to tell everyone about it at your setting the next day.

Cheese hunt

What you need
One A4-sized sheet of black paper; scissors; one piece of white paper 7cm by 5cm; felt-tipped pens

Preparation
Fold the black paper into eight rectangles and cut them out. On the white paper, draw and colour a wedge of cheese, and cut it out.

What to do
Invite eight children to stand in a circle with their arms around each other's shoulders. Explain that the spaces between them are mouse holes and put a rectangle of black paper on the floor in each space. Explain that the two remaining children are going to be mice. Ask the mice to turn their backs for a moment and, while they are not looking, hide the cheese under one of the pieces of paper.

Ask one mouse to pretend to sleep in the centre of the circle while the other mouse scurries in and out of the spaces, lifting up the pieces of paper and looking for the cheese. As the mouse searches, invite everyone to sing to the tune of 'In and Out the Dusky Bluebells' (Traditional):

In and out the little mouse holes
In and out the little mouse holes
In and out the little mouse holes
Looking for the cheese!

Say that the sleeping mouse can wake up just once and creep to only one mouse hole and lift up the paper, looking for the cheese. Explain that it does not matter who finds the cheese first, because both mice are kind and will share the food. When one of the mice has found the cheese, hide it in a different mouse hole, choose two new mice and play again.

Support and extension
Simplify the game for younger children by having just one scurrying mouse. Older children could think of different ways that the mice could move, perhaps trying not to touch any of the children forming the 'mouse holes'.

Further ideas
■ Instead of mice and cheese, have a game where a monkey hunts for a bunch of bananas.
■ Let one child pretend to be a horse, pulling another child in a wheeled truck around some cones.

Hedgehogs in hollows

What you need
A table; adult-sized chair; child-sized chair; three curtains or sheets; small bowl containing six cotton-wool balls.

Preparation
Partially cover the table and chairs with the curtains or sheets, to make them look like hollows at the bottom of trees.

What to do
Sit eight children on the floor in a semi-circle facing the 'tree hollows'. Ask one child to stand behind the tree hollows, holding the bowl of cotton-wool balls. Explain that these are snowflakes. Tell the children who are sitting down that you would like them to pretend to be hedgehogs, preparing to hibernate. Explain that each hedgehog's hollow must be large enough for it to curl up inside and go to sleep for the winter. Call one child at a time, saying, for example, 'Rajiv hedgehog! Time to hibernate! The snow is coming!'.

Ask each child to choose a hollow that is big enough for them to crawl inside. Encourage the child holding the snowflakes to decide whether they have chosen appropriately and, if so, to gently shake the snowflakes on top of the hollow. The hedgehog can now have a go at shaking the snow, as you choose a new hedgehog and play again.

Support and extension
With younger children, instead of using a table and chairs, place three hoops of different sizes flat on the floor. With older children, ask two or three hedgehogs at a time to share the hollows between them.

Further ideas
■ Stand four children in a row, pretending to be trees. Ask them to stand with their legs apart, to make the shape of a tree hollow. Invite one seated child to decide how many hedgehogs could hibernate at a time and encourage them to touch the right number of hedgehogs, each of whom then scurry to a hollow. Change the number of trees each time.
■ Set up a play tunnel and explain that it is a hollow log. Keep changing its length by squashing or extending it, and ask children to estimate how many hedgehogs could fit inside each time, before letting them go inside.

On track

What you need
Chalk (if outside) or tailor's chalk (if inside).

Preparation
Draw a circle in chalk approximately 3m in diameter. Draw three more concentric circles inside the circle, each approximately 45cm apart, to make three tracks (see illustration). If you are doing this activity inside, you can use tailor's chalk on a carpeted area. Arrange three chairs around the edge of the circle for spectators.

What to do
Invite three children to sit on the chairs. Explain that at athletics events, there is always a sports track. Ask each of the three remaining children to stand inside the large circle, each on their own lane. Tell them that you would like them to move around their piece of track in special ways. Explain that they will not be in a race, so there will be no winner, and that you would like everyone to do their best to stay inside their own lane just as real athletes do.

On your signal, ask everyone to jog around their lane. Encourage the spectators to watch carefully to see that no-one steps over their line. If they do, say they will be disqualified. Ask everyone to continue jogging until you say, 'Stop'. If everyone has managed to stay on their track, give them a round of applause. Ask the joggers to sit down and the spectators to replace them.

Support and extension
Ask younger children to walk around their lanes. Older children could walk around their tracks with their arms outstretched and their legs wide apart, in a star shape. Ask them to take care to bring their arms inwards, whenever they feel they might touch someone else.

Further ideas
■ Let the children suggest different ways of moving, such as crawling or hopping.
■ Try moving like different animals, such as elephants (trunks swinging), penguins (waddling) or gorillas (lurching).
■ Encourage the children to push dolls' buggies around the lanes.

Fitness circuit

What you need
Five simple pieces of small apparatus, such as a hoop, beanbag, two quoits, a low bench, two skittles; a cassette or CD player; pop music.

Preparation
Arrange each item at intervals in a circle.

What to do
Tell the children that each item in the circle is an activity station in a fitness circuit at a health club. Invite each child to stand next to a station. Encourage each child to make up their own exercise routine using the item at their station. For example, they could use the skittles as weights. Play the music and enjoy working out! After approximately 50 seconds, turn the volume right down and say, 'Change stations!', encouraging each child to move to the next activity. If using a fitness circuit outside, arrange the items around a chalked circle. If any child has devised an interesting routine, let them demonstrate it to the others. When the children have completed two circuits, ask another five children to replace them.

Support and extension
With younger children, demonstrate a few activities with the items before they begin their circuit. Ask older children for suggestions for other items of equipment that may be used at the stations.

■ ■ ■ ■ ■ ■ ■ ■ ■ ■ ■ ■ ■ ■ ■ ■

Further ideas
■ Let the children help dolls and/or teddy bears to use the fitness circuit.
■ Ask children about any dance or movement clubs they attend. Perhaps they could demonstrate some activities for the other children at your setting to try.
■ Encourage the children to tell you about the facilities at any soft-play centres they visit. Let them make their own versions for play people, using junk items.
■ Ask the children's older brothers and sisters, or parents, to demonstrate their favourite sports or fitness activities at your setting. Encourage them to bring along any special equipment. Take photographs to put inside a 'Keeping fit and healthy' book.

Beach ball challenge

LEARNING OBJECTIVES
STEPPING STONE
Retrieve, collect and catch objects.

EARLY LEARNING GOAL
Use a range of small and large equipment.

GROUP SIZE
Ten children.

What you need
An inflatable beach ball or a large lightweight ball; chairs.

What to do
Arrange ten chairs in a circle, fairly close together. Invite the children to sit on the chairs and explain that you are going to play some ball games. Show the children the inflatable beach ball and ask them to suggest different ways of passing the ball around the circle so that it does not go astray. Begin by simply passing the ball around the circle a few times. Pass it one way around the circle, and then pass it back the other way. Now invite the children to think of other ways that they could pass it. Encourage them to be as imaginative as possible, and to think about using different parts of

their bodies. For example, you could try closing your eyes and carefully passing the ball around, wearing gloves or perhaps putting one arm behind your back and trying to pass the ball one-handed.

Practise different ways of passing the ball, letting different children suggest a technique each time.

Support and extension

HOME LINKS
Encourage parents to help their children develop whole-body co-ordination skills by playing different ball games at home. Ask them to use a range of equipment, including bats, mini golf clubs, netball hoops and footballs to help the children develop a range of skills.

With younger children, use a foam ball that can be gripped easily with smaller hands. With older children, ask everyone to turn their chairs sideways, so they are all facing in the same direction. Ask the children to pass the ball over their heads, either forwards or backwards, or to roll it backwards between their feet, for the person behind to catch.

Further ideas
■ Remove the chairs and ask the children to devise ways of passing the ball standing up.
■ Ask everyone to crouch on their hands and knees, with arms and legs spread apart, and to pass the ball between their legs either forwards or backwards.
■ Use balls of different shapes and sizes, such as a small rugby ball or a ping-pong ball.

Quickly but carefully

What you need
A large threading bead tied to the end of a lace; medium-sized potato; tablespoon; chairs.

What to do
Sit the children on chairs in a circle. Talk about how it is often important to do things quickly but carefully, and how if we rush, we can make mistakes or may even have to start again. Discuss a few examples, such as getting dressed

or cooking. Show the children the bead on the lace and demonstrate how you can make it swing from side to side, just like a pendulum in a clock. Invite the children to play a game where they all work together to do something quickly but very carefully before the pendulum stops swinging. Put the potato on the tablespoon and ask everyone to pass it around the circle quickly but carefully. Start swinging the bead from side to side as the first child passes the potato and spoon to the next child, and enjoy watching it get slower and slower as the potato makes its way around the circle.

Support and extension
Use a small potato and a tablespoon with younger children. Use a large potato and a dessertspoon with older children.

Further ideas
■ Toss bean-bag 'pancakes' from one toy frying pan to another.
■ Ask the children to put on plastic aprons and let them try passing around a plastic cup that is almost full of water.
■ Choose a doll and eight items of loose-fitting clothing that can be put on the doll quickly and easily, such as a vest, pants, socks, jumper, trousers, jacket, hat and scarf. Give one item of clothing to everyone in the circle. Pass around the doll and ask the children to try dressing the doll before the pendulum stops swinging.

LEARNING OBJECTIVES
STEPPING STONE
Use increasing control over an object by touching, pushing, patting, throwing, catching or kicking it.

EARLY LEARNING GOAL
Use a range of small and large equipment.

GROUP SIZE
Eight children.

HOME LINKS
Let each child take home a pendulum made from a ball of silver foil attached to the end of a piece of wool with sticky tape. Ask parents to help their children think of fun challenges to do, such as putting on socks, before the pendulum stops swinging.

Washing circle

What you need
A skipping rope or length of thick string; four items of children's clothing, such as a T-shirt, jumper, shirt and vest; eight spring-action clothes pegs; chairs.

What to do
Arrange the chairs in a circle and ask the children to sit on them. Invite two children sitting opposite one another to hold the ends of the washing line, so that it is taut. Talk about how the sun and wind dry clothes on a washing line, but how sometimes, if it is very windy, the washing line can be blown down. Ask two children to peg two garments each on the washing line. Invite everyone to sing the song below, to the tune of 'Ring-a-ring o' Roses' (Traditional). As everyone sings, ask the children holding the washing line to make it sway from side to side. As you sing the last line of the song, ask the children to gently let the line drop to the floor:

The wind is blowing the clothes high
Up and up in the bright blue sky.
Oh dear! Oh dear!
They've all fallen down!

Ask two different children to hold the washing line, and another two children to unpeg the dirty clothes and mime the action of putting them in the washing machine, before pegging them out again on the washing line.

Support and extension
Use dolly pegs with younger children. Tell older children that sometimes we use just one peg to peg together adjacent garments. Give two children just five pegs between them, and ask them to peg the four garments on the line.

Further ideas
■ Collect items that require a squeezing, pincer hand movement, such as lemon or tea-bag squeezers or tweezers. Let the children practise using these under supervision.
■ Let the children roll out play-dough pastry to cover small dishes. Show them how to pinch the edges of the pie crust.
■ Decorate socks to look like birds. Let the children put their hands in the socks and practise picking up wool 'worms' from a tray, using their fingers and thumbs in a pincer-grip movement.

LEARNING OBJECTIVES
STEPPING STONE
Use one-handed tools and equipment.

EARLY LEARNING GOAL
Handle tools, objects, construction and malleable materials safely and with increasing control.

GROUP SIZE
Any size.

HOME LINKS
Let the children roll small balls of aluminium foil up to make 'diamonds' to take home. Ask families to help their children use tweezers to count the diamonds.

Creative development

This chapter suggests ideas so that children can begin to explore colour, texture, shape and space, recognise how sounds can be changed, sing simple songs from memory, pretend one object represents another, engage in role-play using their imaginations and use body language to communicate.

Colour wheel

What you need
Eight chalks in different colours; eight wax crayons in colours to match the chalks; battery-operated portable cassette player; medium-paced music.

Preparation
Draw a chalk circle on the ground outside, approximately 3m in diameter. Draw eight spokes inside the circle, each in a different colour. Arrange eight chairs around the outside of the circle, approximately 1m away from it, facing inwards (see illustration right).

What to do
Ask the children to sit on the chairs. Give each child a wax crayon in a colour matching a spoke. As you play the music, ask individual children to skip round the outside of the circle. When you stop the music, ask the child to stop skipping. The child should hold up their crayon, say its colour and walk around the circle until they find the spoke in the matching colour. Encourage them to place their crayon on the spoke and sit down. Continue playing until everyone has correctly positioned their crayon on a coloured spoke.

Support and extension
Ask younger children to find the matching spoke, but not necessarily to name the colour. Do not give older children a crayon; instead, ask them to stand on a particular coloured spoke. If they are correct, give them the matching crayon to place upon it.

Further ideas
■ Invite individual children to skip around the circle and to stand on a spoke that matches an item of their clothing.
■ Ask one child to stand with their back to the circle, as everyone else skips round. When the music stops, ask everyone to stand on a spoke (more than one child may stand on the same spoke). Ask the first child to say a colour out loud. Anyone standing on that colour spoke is eliminated. Pick another child to choose a colour and continue until only one child remains.

LEARNING OBJECTIVES
STEPPING STONE
Begin to differentiate colours.

EARLY LEARNING GOAL
Explore colour, texture, shape, form and space in two or three dimensions.

GROUP SIZE
Eight children.

HOME LINKS
Encourage the children to show the colour wheel to the person collecting them and to choose their favourite colour. Ask families to help their children find an item at home in the same colour, to bring to your setting on their next visit. Invite everyone to place their items on the matching spokes at the same time, then take a photograph of your colour wheel.

Colour mixing palette

What you need
Two red hats; one blue hat; one yellow hat; one white hat; one black hat (you can make your own hats or headbands from coloured sugar paper); one palette of red, blue, yellow, white and black block paints; two trays; six paintbrushes; six pieces of white A4 paper; small jug of water.

Preparation
Moisten the paints. Place the palette and brushes on one tray and one piece of paper on the second tray.

What to do
Sit everyone on the floor in a circle. Give all of the children a hat to wear in the following order: red, blue, yellow, red, white and black. Place the paint trays in the centre. Ask the first child wearing the red hat to walk to the child wearing the blue hat, as you all sing the following song to the tune of 'Tommy Thumb' (Traditional):

One, two, three
Come with me!
Let us see
What new colour we can make
What will it be?

Challenge the two children to predict what new colour will be made if they mix their paints. Ask them to walk to the palette, take a brush each and rub it into the paint that is the same colour as their hat. Encourage the red child to paint a blob on the piece of paper, and the blue child to mix their paint into the blob. What colour has been mixed? Let the children offer their suggestions and then sit down.

Now ask the blue child to sing to the yellow child, and continue the game. Keep replacing the pieces of paper and moistening the paints, if necessary. By the end of the game, you should have mixed the following colours: purple, green, orange, pink, grey.

Support and extension
Ask younger children only to paint a blob in their colour and to try naming it. Suggest older children sit randomly. Say, for example, 'Stand up, the two people who think they can make green together', and so on.

Further ideas
■ Hold up coloured objects and challenge the children to mix colours that match them.
■ Let everyone experiment using eye-droppers to drop different colours of food-colouring into plastic tumblers of water.

Quickly, slowly

What you need
One percussion instrument for each child.

What to do
Sit all but one of the children in a circle. Ask the child to stand about a metre away from the circle, facing away from it. Give each child in the circle a percussion instrument and ask them to place it on the floor in front of their feet. Invite everyone to join in with you as you chant, 'Quickly, slowly, loudly, quietly', over and over again. As you chant, ask the standing child to walk slowly around the circle, and to stop wherever they choose. The rest of the group stops chanting at this point. Encourage the child who is sitting at this position to pick up their instrument and to play it quickly, slowly, loudly or quietly, depending on the word reached in the chant at that point. Congratulate the child for playing their instrument, then invite the standing and sitting children to change places before continuing the game.

Support and extension
Ask younger children to chant using only two words (such as, 'Loudly, quietly') at a time. Ask older children to make up alternative chants, for example, 'Slowly, slowly, quickly, loudly'.

Further ideas
■ Ask two adjacent children at a time to stand up. Ask one child to make up a chant for the other child to play and vice-versa.
■ Invite individual volunteers to stand up and say to the group, 'How am I playing?'. Ask them to play either quickly or slowly, loudly or quietly for everyone else to guess.
■ Stand up yourself, and say that you are going to play an instrument, quickly and loudly, or quickly and quietly, or slowly and loudly, or slowly and quietly. Play an instrument and challenge the children to describe how you played it.

LEARNING OBJECTIVES
STEPPING STONE
Explore and learn how sounds can be changed.

EARLY LEARNING GOAL
Recognise and explore how sounds can be changed, sing simple songs from memory, recognise repeated sounds and sound patterns, and match movements to music.

GROUP SIZE
Up to 15 children.

HOME LINKS
Let the children make shakers using a yoghurt pot, dried beans and a paper top, attached securely with sticky tape or a rubber band. Invite the children to take them home to play quickly or slowly, loudly or quietly.

Oh Joe!

What you need
One soft toy or plastic elephant, monkey, snake and tiger; tray.

What to do
Sit down together in a circle, and say the traditional rhyme 'Mary Had a Little Lamb'. Hold up the animals and explain that they are all called 'Joe'. Invite everyone to make up a rhyme about any Joe, following them to school. Put the animals on a tray in the centre space, then ask one child to choose an animal and hold it. Invite everyone to say the rhyme below, as the child holds the animal:

> (Chloe) had a little (snake)
> And its name was Joe.
> Everywhere that (Chloe) went
> Joe was sure to go!
> He followed Chloe to school one day
> And…

Ask the children to stop speaking at that point, and encourage the child holding the animal to say what happened. Ask the child to replace their animal on the tray. Continue playing, inviting the next child to choose an animal.

Support and extension
Do not ask younger children what happened; conclude the song each time with the words 'That was against the rule. It made the children laugh and play to see a (snake) at school!'. After playing the game with older children, ask them to complete the 'Fill the gaps' photocopiable sheet on page 79. Ask each child to write their name in the rectangles, and to choose an animal to write in the space. At the bottom of each sheet, write down each child's ending.

Further ideas
■ Ask the children if they can suggest any other animals that could follow them to school.
■ Let children use small-world furniture, play-people and a model animal to show what happened at the end of the rhyme.

Wriggle and tickle

What you need
One adult-sized plain sock for each child; tambourine.

What to do
Sit everyone in a circle. Give each of the children a sock, and invite them to put it on one hand, pretending that it is a garden worm. Encourage everyone to join in with the following rhyme, making appropriate movements:

> *Round and round the garden*
> *Worms go everywhere*
> *One wriggle, two wriggle*
> *Tickle you under there!*

On the last line, ask each child to gently tickle the child next to them. Encourage each pair of children to practise mirroring each other's 'worm' movements. Then invite each pair to demonstrate their mirroring, as you play the tambourine.

Support and extension
Encourage younger children to pass around a medium-sized potato from worm to worm. Ask each pair of older children to make up a simple story about two worms having an adventure in a garden. Invite them to tell their adventure to the rest of the group.

Further ideas
■ Ask individual children wearing a 'worm sock' to crawl on their tummy to collect paper leaves to eat. Encourage them to count how many leaves they have collected.
■ Stuff a sock with paper and tie the end with string. Tie another piece of string approximately 50cm long to the same end. Draw a wiggly line on the carpet with tailor's chalk, and invite individual children to pull the worm along the line.
■ Let two children play 'Worms and worm holes'. Ask one child to make finger holes in damp sand and tell them that these are worm holes, and that one worm lives in each hole. Explain that the holes are empty because each worm has gone looking for leaves. Ask the second child to say how many worms are missing and to fill each hole with a worm (a piece of straw) when they come back home.

LEARNING OBJECTIVES
STEPPING STONE
Pretend that one object represents another, especially when objects have characteristics in common.

EARLY LEARNING GOAL
Use their imagination in art and design, music, dance, imaginative and role-play and stories.

GROUP SIZE
Up to 12 children.

HOME LINKS
Ask families to send in plain adult-sized socks for the children to make into 'magic worm' glove puppets. Let each child stick on two peel-off circular labels for eyes. Stick a strip of double-sided tape along the back of the worm, and encourage the children to stick on small pieces of crêpe and metallic paper.

Round the seasons

LEARNING OBJECTIVES
STEPPING STONE
Engage in imaginative and role-play based on own first-hand experiences.

EARLY LEARNING GOAL
Use their imagination in art and design, music, dance, imaginative and role-play and stories.

GROUP SIZE
12 children.

What you need
One copy of the 'Season cycle' photocopiable sheet on page 80; scissors; tray; seasonal props (optional): Spring – a kite (home-made or bought); Summer – small picnic blanket, two plastic cups, play food; Autumn – real or paper leaves, a small net curtain; Winter – cotton-wool balls, a small net curtain.

Preparation
Cut out the pictures on the photocopiable sheet and place them on the tray.

What to do
Ask everyone to sit in a circle on the floor. Say the rhyme on the photocopiable sheet together, as everyone passes the tray around the circle. When you have finished saying the rhyme, ask the child holding the tray to point to the spring picture. Encourage the child to stand up and move into the centre of the circle, and to pretend to be a tree. Ask two other children to role-play a scenario where the kite gets stuck in the tree on a blustery spring day. If you are not using props, the children can mime the scenario.

Continue the game, acting out a scenario for each of the seasons. If you are using props for autumn and winter, you could ask the children pretending to be the trees to kneel down while the others gently shake the leaves or snowflakes from the net on top of them.

Support and extension
Guide younger children in acting out a season by providing a running commentary on the scene. Ask older children for alternative ideas for seasonal activities to act out, for example, looking for a lost lamb in springtime (and so on).

Further ideas
■ Encourage individual children to give weather reports. Challenge the rest of the group to listen carefully in order to guess which season they are reporting on.
■ Let the children sit on the floor and use glove puppets to act out a scenario from each season.
■ Cut out seasonal pictures from calendars and magazines to talk about with the children.

HOME LINKS
Invite parents and carers to watch the children's role-play, and to try the activity at home.

Mystery train

What you need
One train driver's hat.

What to do
Choose one child to be an engine driver and give them the hat to wear. Ask everyone else to stand in a queue behind the driver, pretending to be train carriages. Encourage the children to move the train into a circular shape, leaving a gap between the driver and the last carriage. Ask everyone to position their arms loosely at either side of the person in front of them, conga style. Tell the children that sometimes, people like to go on a mystery train journey, where only one or two people (including the driver, of course!) know the destination. Explain that in this game only the driver knows the destination.

Ask the driver to start the engine and encourage everyone to move round in a circle, like a train. As you move, invite everyone to sing the following song to the tune of 'The Big Ship Sails on the Alley-Alley-O' (Traditional).

> *We're all going on a tra–in today.*
> *A train today, a train today,*
> *We're all going on a tra–in today,*
> *But we don't know where!*

When you have finished singing, sit down in your circle. Ask the driver to say, 'We're at…', adding the name of the place where they have chosen to take everyone. Prompt the children by talking about enjoyable activities, such as going to the beach, zoo or funfair. Ask another child to be the driver and play again.

Support and extension
With younger children ask the driver to whisper their chosen destination to you. Suggest a destination if necessary. With older children, ask the driver to mime enjoyable activities at the destination, for everyone to guess and copy.

Further ideas
■ Play 'I spy on the way'. Ask for volunteers to think of something that they might see on a train journey, and say, 'I spy with my little eye something on the way beginning with…'.
■ Encourage the children to use small-world and junk items to create destinations such as the seaside, a mountain area, a forest or a castle, which can be placed alongside their toy train track.

LEARNING OBJECTIVES
STEPPING STONE
Introduce a story line or narrative into their play.

EARLY LEARNING GOAL
Use their imagination in art and design, music, dance, imaginative and role-play and stories.

GROUP SIZE
Up to 12 children.

HOME LINKS
Ask families to send in leaflets about popular places of interest. Stick them into a 'Special journeys' book.

Who can it be?

What you need
A cassette or CD player; medium-paced music.

What to do
Gather everyone together in a circle on the floor. Sit down in the centre of the circle and describe out loud each of the children's hairstyles and clothes in turn. Say, for example, 'I can see Zara's two bunches and two flower bobbles in her hair, and her velvet dress and tall boots'. Ask another adult to play the music, and then encourage everyone to crawl around in a circle on their hands and knees. While the music is playing and the children are crawling around, close your eyes tightly.

When the music stops, ask everyone to stop where they are and sit back down in the circle. Keep your eyes closed and shuffle towards one of the child. Gently touch their hair and clothes, identifying the features and describing what you feel. For example, 'You have spiky hair today. It feels tickly. You have a fleece. It feels soft and cuddly. I think you are Lewis!'.

Invite a child to replace you in the centre of the circle. Encourage them to look carefully at everyone's hair and clothes, then tell them to close their eyes. Play the music, and invite everyone to crawl around as before. Ask the child to touch someone, describe how their hair and clothes feel, and then go on to try and name them.

Support and extension
Play with just three younger children at a time. Extend the group size to six with older children.

Further ideas
■ Play the game again, this time wearing outdoor clothing.
■ Provide a selection of different dolls, teddy bears and soft toys. Play the game again, this time asking just one child at a time to close their eyes as the music plays, and hand them a toy to describe for when the music stops. Remind them that they must keep their eyes shut!
■ Let children play 'Guess who' games by touching legs and shoes only.

You'll never guess!

What you need
One baby doll for every child in the group; one plastic mirror for each child (optional); chairs.

What to do
Sit everyone on chairs in a circle. Talk about how babies can make grown-ups and older children feel amused. Say that sometimes they can make people feel tired, especially when they keep doing something, such as repeatedly throwing toys out of their buggy. Explain that people can often find out how

somebody else is feeling by looking at the expression on their face. Pretend to look amused and tired, and see if the children can read your facial expression. Ask the children to practise looking amused and tired using the mirrors (if available).

Give everyone a doll to hold. Encourage each child to choose whether to look amused or tired. Say to each child in turn, 'You're looking amused today… (name of child). Can you tell me why?'. Ask each child to reply, 'Yes, you'll never guess what my baby did! She…'. Invite the child to finish the sentence, explaining why they feel amused.

Support and extension
Encourage younger children to talk about what makes their baby feel amused or tired. Ask older children to talk about when members of their family look amused and tired, and why this might be.

Further ideas
■ Encourage children to think of other facial expressions. Invite each child in turn to make an expression, and challenge the rest of the group to say how they think the child is feeling. Let the child say whether they are correct, and talk about the circumstances that would make them feel that way.
■ Look at the faces of characters in books and ask children to say how they think the characters are feeling.
■ Let children talk about the expressions on the faces of some dolls, play-people and toy animals at your setting.

LEARNING OBJECTIVES
STEPPING STONE
Use body language, gestures, facial expression or words to indicate personal satisfaction or frustration.

EARLY LEARNING GOAL
Express and communicate their ideas, thoughts and feelings by using a widening range of materials, suitable tools, imaginative and role-play, movement, designing and making, and a variety of songs and musical instruments.

GROUP SIZE
Up to ten children.

HOME LINKS
Make photocopied slips of the following rhyme for the children to take home. Ask them to play 'Guess my expression' games with family members.
How am I feeling today?
Look at my face and it will say!

Dream catcher

What you need

One medium-sized hoop; four lengths of thick wool, each approximately 80cm long, and four lengths each approximately 130cm long; sticky tape.

Preparation

Attach the four 80cm lengths of wool to the hoop with sticky tape in a criss-cross pattern (see illustration below).

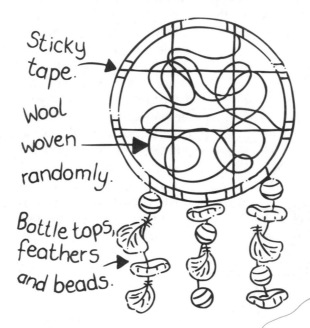

Sticky tape.

Wool woven randomly.

Bottle tops, feathers and beads.

What to do

Sit the children on the floor in a circle. Explain that in North America, the Native Americans make dream catchers, which are hoops with beautiful patterns threaded inside with string or wool, like spiders' webs. Tell the children that, long ago, Native Americans hung dream catchers outside their tepees at night. They thought that happy dreams would pass through the web into the tepees for the people to dream about, and unhappy dreams would be caught in the webs until morning, when they would vanish. With each child, attach one end of their wool to the hoop with sticky tape, and let them loosely weave their wool to make a web. As each child works, chat together about their dreams, and yours.

Support and extension

Ask younger children what they would like to dream about. Ask older children to talk about any dreams that remind them of real things that have happened to them.

Further ideas

■ Suspend the dream catcher and attach three lengths of wool, each approximately 30cm long, to the bottom of the hoop. Decorate these with beads, feathers or milk bottle tops.

■ Using two animal glove puppets – a baby and a mother or father – pretend to be the baby animal yourself, and say you have just woken up from a slightly unhappy dream. Ask a child to use the mother or father glove puppet to cuddle the baby glove puppet and talk to you about the dream, to make you feel better again.

How is Teddy?

(Tune: 'If You're Happy and You Know It')

What makes Teddy
happy, sad or cross?

What makes Teddy
happy, sad or cross?

What makes him happy?
What makes him sad?

What makes him cross?
Let's find out!

Linda Mort

Festival facts

At _____ people may...

greet people

eat special food

do special things

pray

How do you feel?

Ask the children to draw in the dog's tail to show how it is feeling.

happy

sad

playful

Sing a song (1)

Red Riding Hood

(Tune: 'There Was a Princess Long Ago')

Red Riding Hood put on her cloak, put on her cloak, put on her cloak
Red Riding Hood put on her cloak – yes, she did!
Mummy filled a basket with food...
Red Riding Hood went into the forest...
The big, bad wolf hid behind a tree...
Then the wolf talked to her...
The wolf ran off to Grandma's cottage...
The wolf put Grandma in the wardrobe...
Then the wolf climbed into bed...
Red Riding Hood knocked on the door...
Red Riding Hood spoke to the wolf...
The wolf chased her round and round...
Daddy came and rescued her...
Then the wolf ran away...
Then they let Grandma out...
Then they had a lovely tea... – yes, they did!

Linda Mort

Sing a song (2)

Jack and the Beanstalk

(Tune: 'There Was a Princess Long Ago')

Once there was a boy called Jack, a boy called Jack, a boy called Jack
Once there was a boy called Jack, yes, there was!
One day he took the cow to market...
On the way, he met a man...
The man gave Jack some magic beans...
Mum was cross and threw them away...
The beans grew high into the sky...
Next day Jack climbed up and up...
Jack knocked and knocked on the big brown door...
The giant's wife opened the door...
Then she hid Jack inside the oven...
The great big giant came stamping in...
The giant started to count the money...
Then the giant fell fast asleep...
Jack took the money and ran down the beanstalk...
The giant ran after him straight away...
Jack asked mum for an axe...
Jack chopped and chopped the beanstalk down...
The giant fell down and down...
Yes, he did!

Linda Mort

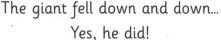

If..., page 22

Can you guess?

Rhyme time

Teddy's team

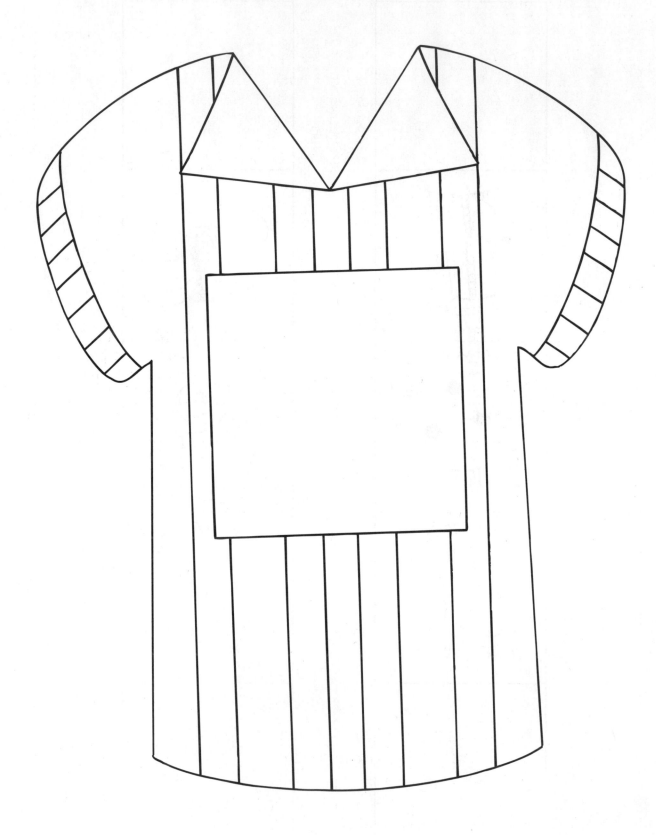

Count the quacks!

Invite the children to count out the correct number of cubes of bread.

Silkworm song

(Tune: 'Here We Go Round the Mulberry Bush')

We are little silkworms, silkworms, silkworms.
We are little silkworms wriggling round a mulberry bush.

This is the way we munch the leaves,
munch the leaves, munch the leaves.
This is the way we munch the leaves,
yes, we do!

Now we are very big, very big, very big.
Now we are very big,
yes, we are!

Now we spin a cocoon of thread,
a cocoon of thread, a cocoon of thread.
Now we spin a cocoon of thread,
yes, we do!

Now we've turned into a moth
into a moth, into a moth.
Now we've turned into a moth,
yes, we have!

Linda Mort

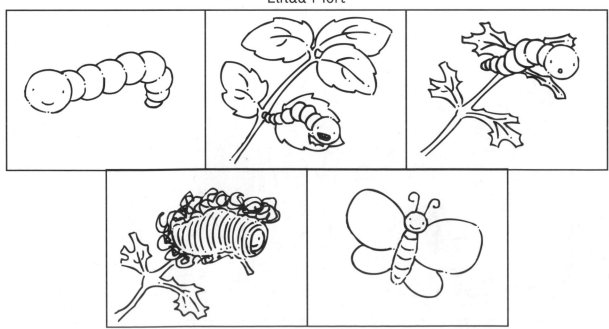

Can we help?

Teddy's journey

(Tune: 'The Bear Went Over the Mountain')

Teddy went over the bridge
The bridge, the bridge
Teddy went over the bridge
To try and find his key.

Teddy went to the playground...
Teddy went to the Post Office...
Teddy went to the car wash...
Teddy went to the station...

Teddy went back to his garden,
His garden, his garden.
Teddy went back to his garden
And there he found his key!

Linda Mort

Fill the gaps

Name:

Date:

[   ] had a little

_____ and its name

was Joe. [   ]

Everywhere that

went, Joe was sure to go!

[   ]

He followed

to school one day

and...

Season cycle

Spring, summer, autumn, winter!
Spring, summer, autumn, winter!
Every season has something new
And lots of things for us to do!
Spring, summer, autumn, winter!
Spring, summer, autumn, winter!

Linda Mort